THE IN-DEPTH JAPAN TRAVEL GUIDE 2023-2024

Budget Travel Japan That Will Blow Your Mind, The Weirdest Modern Country Hidden Gems & Off-The-Beaten-Track Locations for Your Next Trip

GEORGIA TUCKER

Georgia Tucker

COPYRIGHT

No part of this book may be reproduced in any written, electronic, recording, or photocopying without written permission of the publisher or author.

The exception would be in the case of brief quotations embodied in the critical articles or reviews and pages where permission is specifically granted by the publisher or author.

Although every precaution has been taken to verify the accuracy of the information contained herein, the author and publisher assume no responsibility for any errors or omissions. No liability is assumed for damages that may result from the use of the information contained within.

All Right Reserved©2023

Georgia Tucker

Georgia Tucker

TABLE OF CONTENTS

TABLE OF CONTENTS	2
INTRODUCTION	6
WELCOME TO JAPAN	6
WHY TRAVEL TO JAPAN? 20 BEST REASONS TO VISIT IT	9
CHAPTER ONE	20
A BRIEF HISTORY OF JAPAN	20
HOW TO PLAN YOUR TRIP TO JAPAN	22
BEST TIME TO VISIT JAPAN	23
CHAPTER TWO	30
DISCOVERING KYOTO	30
WELCOME TO KYOTO	30
TOP THINGS TO SEE AND DO IN KYOTO	31
KYOTO TRAVEL COSTS AND BUDGET	38
MONEY-SAVING TIPS	43
WHERE TO STAY IN KYOTO	46
HOW TO GET AROUND KYOTO	47
WHEN TO GO TO KYOTO	49
HOW TO STAY SAFE IN KYOTO	50
CHAPTER THREE	54

GREAT ITINARY IDEAS	**54**
HOW TO BUDGET AND SAVE MONEY TIPS	**84**
A GUIDE TO DAILY COSTS IN JAPAN	**90**
22 WONDERFUL THINGS TO DO IN JAPAN	**91**

CHAPTER FOUR   108

DISCOVERING TOKYO	**108**
WELCOME TO TOKYO	**108**
THINGS TO DO IN TOKYO	**109**
WHERE TO EAT IN TOKYO	**113**
THE 10 BEST HOSTELS IN TOKYO	**117**
PLACES TO VISIT IN TOKYO	**129**

CHAPTER FIVE   136

TRANSPORTATION	**136**
HOW TO GET TO AND AROUND JAPAN?	**136**

CHAPTER SIX   146

MUST-TRY LOCAL JAPANESE FOODS	**146**
15 TYPES OF RESTAURANTS IN JAPAN THAT ARE GREAT FOR TOURISTS	
	162

CHAPTER SEVEN   168

DISCOVERING HOKKAIDO	**168**
WELCOME TO HOKKAIDO	**168**
THE BEST THINGS TO DO IN HOKKAIDO	**168**
THE 10 BEST HOTELS IN HOKKAIDO	**184**

15 BEST PLACES TO VISIT IN HOKKAIDO	191
20 RESTAURANTS IN HOKKAIDO TO TRY ITS MANY DELICACIES	202

CHAPTER EIGHT — 228

ACCOMMODATION IN JAPAN	228
SHOPPING IN JAPAN	237

CHAPTER NINE — 246

LANGUAGE AND COMMUNICATION IN JAPAN	246
JAPANESE CULTURE AND TRADITION	253
LANGUAGE BARRIERS IN JAPAN? TRAVEL IN JAPAN WITHOUT SPEAKING JAPANESE	273
USEFUL JAPANESE EXPRESSIONS WHILE TRAVELING IN JAPAN	275

CHAPTER TEN — 280

THE TOP 10 TOURIST ATTRACTIONS IN JAPAN	280
GREAT OUTDOOR ACTIVITIES IN JAPAN	290
THE TOP 10 BEACHES IN JAPAN	294

CHAPTER ELEVEN — 308

SAFETY IN JAPAN	308
16 TIPS FOR HOW TO SAVE MONEY IN JAPAN WHEN TRAVELLING JAPAN!	314

CONCLUSION — 322

Georgia Tucker

Georgia Tucker

Georgia Tucker

INTRODUCTION

WELCOME TO JAPAN

Welcome to "The In-Depth Japan Travel Guide 2023-2024," your ultimate resource for planning a memorable and affordable trip to one of the world's most fascinating countries. This guide is designed to help you discover the best that Japan has to offer, from its vibrant cities and ancient temples to its stunning natural landscapes and quirky, off-the-beaten-track destinations.

We know that travel can be expensive, which is why this guide is focused on budget travel options that won't break the bank. But don't worry, just because we're keeping costs low doesn't mean we're skimping on the experience. We're going to take you to some of the weirdest, most interesting places in Japan that you won't find in your typical tourist guidebook.

So why Japan? It's a country that's both modern and steeped in tradition, with a unique culture that's unlike any other in the world. It's a place where the latest technology and ancient customs coexist in perfect harmony. It's a country of contrasts, where you can ski on world-class slopes in the morning and soak in a hot spring in the afternoon. And with a culture that values hospitality and politeness above all else, you're sure to feel welcome wherever you go.

This guide will take you through the must-see sights of Tokyo and Kyoto, but it will also introduce you to the hidden gems of Japan that are often overlooked by tourists. You'll discover the quirky, offbeat neighbourhoods of Tokyo, like Harajuku and Shimokitazawa, where you can find the latest fashion trends and street food. You'll explore the ancient capital of Nara, where deer roam freely through the streets and centuries-old temples and shrines stand side by side. You'll also visit the stunning natural landscapes of Hokkaido and Okinawa, where you can hike through forests, dive in crystal-clear waters, and soak in hot springs surrounded by snow.

We've done our research and scoured the country to find the best budget travel options, from affordable accommodations and delicious street food to free attractions and hidden gems that won't cost you a dime. We've also included practical tips for navigating Japan's transportation system, getting the most out of your yen, and avoiding common tourist traps.

So, whether you're a first-time visitor or a seasoned Japan traveller looking for something new and off the beaten track, "The In-Depth Japan Travel Guide 2023-2024" has something for everyone. Get ready to experience a Japan that will blow your mind, and create memories that will last a lifetime.

WHY TRAVEL TO JAPAN? 20 BEST REASONS TO VISIT IT

Japan presents an array of captivating reasons to visit, catering to a wide range of traveller preferences. Whether it's delving into Japanese history and culture through the numerous UNESCO World Heritage Sites, indulging in the diverse culinary offerings, or embarking on a thrilling ride aboard the lightning-fast Shinkansen trains, a journey to Japan promises endless adventure at every turn. Discover the 20 most compelling reasons to consider a visit to this remarkable country.

Georgia Tucker

It's Easy to Get Around On Public Transportation

Japan boasts one of the world's most efficient and dependable public transportation systems, encompassing a comprehensive network of buses, trains, and subways that seamlessly connect various regions across the nation. Among the notable modes of travel is the iconic Shinkansen bullet train, renowned for its extraordinary speed of up to 300 km/h and luxurious amenities. Securing a JR Pass online before arrival offers a cost-effective means of experiencing the Shinkansen.

Japan Is Very Clean

The Japanese people take immense pride in maintaining cleanliness, a characteristic evident from the moment of arrival. Immaculate streets, pristine hotels, and spotless restaurants permeate the surroundings, exuding pleasant aromas and meticulous cleanliness. Although public spaces may lack trash cans, adopting the Japanese practice of carrying waste until suitable disposal options arise is an effective solution.

Japanese People Are Polite and Friendly

Renowned for their extraordinary politeness, friendliness, and warm hospitality, the Japanese have garnered a global reputation. Despite potential language barriers, locals often strive to be accommodating when approached for assistance. Familiarizing oneself with Japanese etiquette before the journey demonstrates respect for local customs and garners appreciation from the locals.

The Incredible Natural Landscapes

While Japan is internationally acclaimed for its technologically advanced cities, the majority of the country is graced by vast expanses of forested hills and mountains, offering abundant opportunities to immerse oneself in nature's wonders. Iconic Mount Fuji stands as a prominent natural gem, yet venturing beyond unveils hidden treasures like the ethereal Arashiyama bamboo forest and the captivating Ritsurin landscape gardens on Shikoku Island.

The Large Number of Unesco Sites

Japan proudly embraces 21 distinguished UNESCO World Heritage Sites, including 17 cultural monuments and 4 natural landscapes, with an additional 8 sites awaiting recognition. History enthusiasts are particularly drawn to the Hiroshima Peace Memorial, a poignant tribute to the victims of the 1945 atomic bomb, as well as the unique thatched-roof dwellings of Shirakawago and Gokayama's historic villages.

The Majestic Temples in Japan

Throughout Japan, an abundance of resplendent historic temples and shrines grace towns and cities alike, while cultural hubs may house up to 1,000 within their municipality. Noteworthy examples include the timeless Byodoin Buddhist temple in Uji, a UNESCO World Heritage Site dating back over a millennium. Additionally, the Toji temple in Kyoto captivates visitors with its towering wooden pagoda, the tallest in Japan, and a sprawling garden adorned with cherry trees.

Georgia Tucker

The Unique Castles

Exploring the refined architectural marvels and captivating historical legacies of Japanese castles allows visitors to delve deep into the rich tapestry of Japan's past. During the Sengoku period, these castles primarily served as the residences of local feudal lords and their families, boasting elegant exteriors, opulent interiors, and formidable defensive structures.

Among the most impressive castles in Japan, Hikone Castle, dating back to 1622, stands as a well-preserved testament to the country's architectural heritage, while the castle in Himeji is a sight to behold.

The Spectacular Cherry Blossom Season

Japan occupies a coveted position as one of the world's finest destinations for experiencing the enchanting springtime cherry blossoms and immersing oneself in Cherry blossom festivals.

As the cherry blossom season reaches its peak in April, both locals and visitors flock to Japanese parks and gardens, indulging in hanami, and picnics beneath the blooming cherry trees. Hirosaki Castle Park and Shinjuku Gyoen, nestled in the heart of Tokyo, rank among the top locations for embracing the ephemeral beauty of these delicate flowers.

The Exciting Summer Festivals

A visit to Japan during the summer months presents an unparalleled opportunity to partake in the vibrant Matsuri festivals that burst with color and exuberance across the nation.

These traditional celebrations pay homage to legendary historical events and deities associated with specific shrines in the respective towns. Many Matsuri festivals feature grand processions of elaborate floats, vivid parades, and awe-inspiring fireworks displays.

Georgia Tucker

Christmas In Japan Is Magical

Immersing oneself in the Christmas festivities in Japan promises a memorable experience, particularly due to the abundance of extravagant winter illuminations that bedeck the city streets during this joyous season.

For those venturing to Japan during the winter months, a visit to the Sapporo Snow Festival in Hokkaido is highly recommended, offering a captivating showcase of intricate ice sculptures, often inspired by beloved pop culture characters.

The World-Class Powder Snow

Winter sports enthusiasts should not miss the opportunity to partake in snowboarding and skiing in Japan, as the country's powder snow is revered as some of the finest in the world.

A multitude of exceptional ski resorts can be found across the country, with Hokkaido's northernmost island serving as home to renowned destinations such as Furano, Rusutsu, and Niseko. The Japanese Alps on Honshu also offer remarkable skiing experiences.

The Chance to Bathe In A Natural Hot Spring

Onsens, Japanese hot spring baths filled with mineral-rich water heated by geothermal forces, provide a serene and rejuvenating bathing experience akin to a natural Jacuzzi.

With a history dating back to at least the 8th century, when hot springs were revered for their curative and revitalizing properties, onsens have become a beloved pastime for both Japanese locals and tourists seeking utmost relaxation.

The Superb Japanese Cuisine

Japanese cuisine holds immense cultural significance, and while in Japan, you will have the opportunity to savor an extensive array of delectable dishes that define its culinary landscape. From globally cherished delicacies like sushi and ramen to traditional delights such as Sukiyaki (beef hot pot) and Yakiniku (Japanese barbecue), Japan presents an infinite gastronomic journey to tantalize your taste buds.

Moreover, Japan boasts the highest number of three-star Michelin restaurants worldwide, and a myriad of Matsuri food and drink festivals allow visitors to partake in unique culinary experiences throughout their trip.

The Fantastic Architecture

While exploring major Japanese cities, prepare to be captivated by the awe-inspiring modern architecture, with iconic landmarks like the Tokyo Skytree, the tallest building in the capital, leaving a lasting impression. Traditional Japanese architecture is equally enchanting, with exquisite examples found across the country, such as the majestic Ise shrines located on the Shima Peninsula.

The Advanced Technology

Japan proudly showcases its advanced technology in every corner of its cities, with futuristic capsule hotels offering complimentary tablets and high-tech public toilets exemplifying the nation's commitment to innovation. To gain deeper insights into Japan's technological advancements, a visit to Miraikan - The National Museum of Emerging Science and Innovation in Tokyo's Odaiba district provides a remarkable opportunity to explore permanent robotics exhibitions.

Japan Is a Mecca For Manga And Anime Lovers

For those whose love for Japan was kindled by manga and anime, Tokyo stands as a veritable paradise, offering a multitude of anime-themed experiences to indulge in.

J-World Tokyo, an indoor amusement park centered around popular manga characters, the One Piece Tower, and the Pokémon Mega Center Tokyo, an expansive store boasting exclusive Pokémon merchandise, provide unparalleled delights for enthusiasts seeking an immersive manga and anime adventure.

It's The Home of Studio Ghibli

Devotees of revered Japanese animated films, such as Princess Mononoke (1997) and Spirited Away (2001), are urged not to miss the opportunity to immerse themselves in the enchanting world of director Hayao Miyazaki's creations at the esteemed Studio Ghibli Museum in Mitaka. From Mitaka Station, the presence of Totoro will guide visitors on their journey, leading them to encounter a colossal replica of the Catbus from My Neighbor Totoro (1988) and exclusive animated shorts showcased solely within the museum's walls. Additionally, a dynamic array of exhibitions continuously delves into the depths of Ghibli's creative process.

Japan Is the Birthplace of Karaoke

Enthusiasts who revel in unleashing their vocal prowess upon an audience, whether comprised of close acquaintances or a gathering of unfamiliar faces, will find solace in Japan's thriving karaoke culture. It is worth noting that karaoke, with its current prevalence of approximately 100,000 karaoke boxes and bars nationwide, originated in Japan. Immerse yourself in this vibrant form of entertainment while in the country, and seize the opportunity to create unforgettable musical memories.

The Fashion

Fashion aficionados embarking on a journey to Japan are advised to direct their steps towards the epitome of sartorial elegance, Harajuku, located in Tokyo. This vibrant neighborhood serves as the nucleus for Japan's foremost trendsetters, where an array of influential establishments awaits. Alternatively, those with a penchant for traditional Japanese fashion may find solace in Kyoto, where the city's renowned kimonos and yukatas invite visitors to partake in an immersive experience of timeless elegance.

Japan Is Very Safe

Renowned as one of the safest nations on the globe, Japan boasts an exceptionally low crime rate. A testament to this safety is observed through Japanese locals' propensity to leave their doors unlocked, the independence of children confidently navigating the subway system unaccompanied, and the ability for visitors to traverse city streets during nocturnal hours without apprehension. Nonetheless, it is prudent for travelers to exercise caution in crowded areas and employ common sense, as one would when visiting any foreign destination.

CHAPTER ONE

A BRIEF HISTORY OF JAPAN

The history of Japan spans thousands of years, beginning with the prehistoric Jomon and Yayoi cultures, and continuing through the rise of feudalism, the Meiji Restoration, and the country's modernization in the 20th century.

The Jomon period, from around 14,000 BCE to 300 BCE, is characterized by a hunter-gatherer lifestyle and the creation of distinctive pottery. The Yayoi period, from around 300 BCE to 300 CE, saw the introduction of rice agriculture and iron tools, as well as the emergence of social stratification and the establishment of a centralized state.

In the 8th century, Japan's imperial court was established in Kyoto, ushering in a period of cultural flourishing and the development of a distinctive Japanese culture. This era was also marked by the rise of powerful regional clans, including the Taira and Minamoto.

The 12th century saw the beginning of the feudal era, with the establishment of the Kamakura shogunate by the Minamoto clan. The shogunate was later replaced by the Ashikaga shogunate in the 14th century, which oversaw a period of cultural and artistic achievement known as the Muromachi period.

In the 16th century, Japan was united under the rule of Oda Nobunaga, Toyotomi Hideyoshi, and Tokugawa Ieyasu, who established the Tokugawa shogunate and implemented strict isolationist policies. The country remained largely closed off from the outside world until the mid-19th century when pressure from foreign powers led to the Meiji Restoration and the modernization of Japan.

The 20th century saw Japan emerge as a global economic and military power, culminating in its defeat in World War II and the subsequent U.S. occupation. In the postwar period, Japan rebuilt its economy and established itself as a leading technological and cultural innovator, while also grappling with the legacy of its imperial past. Today, Japan is a constitutional monarchy with a highly developed economy and a rich cultural heritage.

Japan Today

Today, Japan is a highly developed country and one of the world's largest economies, with a population of around 126 million people. It is known for its technological advancements, high standard of living, and distinctive culture.

Japan's government is a parliamentary democracy with a constitutional monarchy, and the Emperor serves as a largely ceremonial figurehead. The country is divided into 47 prefectures, each with its governor and elected assembly.

The Japanese economy is dominated by industries such as automotive manufacturing, electronics, and telecommunications. The country is also a major exporter of cultural products, including anime, manga, and video games.

In recent years, Japan has faced challenges such as an aging population, a declining birth rate, and economic stagnation. The government has implemented various policies to address these issues, such as promoting women's participation in the workforce and encouraging immigration.

Japan is also known for its distinctive cultural traditions, including tea ceremonies, calligraphy, and martial arts such as judo and karate. The country is home to numerous UNESCO World Heritage sites, including ancient temples and shrines, and hosts a variety of festivals and events throughout the year.

Overall, Japan remains a unique and fascinating country with a rich history, a dynamic present, and a promising future.

HOW TO PLAN YOUR TRIP TO JAPAN

Japan, a highly sought-after destination for many travelers, holds particular appeal for families with teenagers and retired couples. Apart from its captivating blend of nature, history, and modernity, Japan's vibrant and distinctive culture, encompassing sumo, samurai, anime, and sushi, continues to fascinate and entice curious visitors from around the globe.

This book aims to provide a comprehensive guide for planning a trip to Japan, covering essential aspects such as budgeting, ideal times to visit, top destinations, transportation options, and more.

Do I Need a Visa To Visit Japan?

Citizens of numerous countries, including the United States, Canada, the United Kingdom, and Australia, are exempt from obtaining a visa to enter Japan. Most travelers can enjoy a visa-free stay of up to 90 days.

BEST TIME TO VISIT JAPAN

While Japan can be visited throughout the year, each season offers distinct advantages and considerations:

March to May: These months provide the most pleasant weather, making it an ideal time for travel. Spring, in particular, is renowned for its comfortable temperatures and the enchanting spectacle of cherry blossoms in bloom.

June to August: This period offers lower prices and reduced crowds. Many travelers opt to avoid Japan during these months due to the high temperatures (averaging 32°C/90°F) and humidity. Consequently, accommodation and flight prices tend to be more affordable. Summer also coincides with numerous festivals, providing opportunities to immerse oneself in local celebrations and witness mesmerizing fireworks displays. For further ideas on planning a summer trip to Japan, please refer to additional resources.

September to November: This season boasts cool and dry weather, along with fewer tourists. Visitors during this period can enjoy the breathtaking autumn foliage, which paints the countryside near Kyoto and Tokyo in vivid hues of orange and red. It is also an excellent time to explore Japan's renowned national parks, including Mount Fuji and the Five Lakes region.

December to February: For those seeking snow-covered landscapes and winter activities such as skiing, this is the ideal time to visit. Winter in Japan offers the opportunity to experience the tranquility of a ryokan, traditional Japanese inns featuring natural hot springs. Immersing oneself in hot pools amidst snow-covered, serene forests is a truly unforgettable experience. It's important to note that the Christmas/New Year holiday period is particularly busy, with hotels and flights often fully booked. Therefore, it is advisable to plan and secure reservations well in advance. We are dedicated to tailoring your trip to align with your interests and requirements, ensuring a seamless experience.

How Much Does a Japanese Vacation Cost?

Compared to China or Southeast Asian countries, travel in Japan entails higher costs in line with European living standards and service quality. Typically, a private tour with 4-star hotels for a group of 2-4 people amounts to around US$400 (and above) per person per day. This encompasses a private guide, transportation, a comprehensive itinerary, attraction tickets, and accommodations in local 4-star hotels. Opting for a local 5-star hotel would require an additional $100 or more per day.

It is essential to note that March to May is the busiest travel month in Japan, resulting in higher travel costs and increased crowds compared to other times of the year. Therefore, booking flights and hotels well in advance is highly recommended. To secure the services of a professional tour guide for your dream trip in Japan, it is advisable to book a Japan tour at least 6 months before your departure date.

Certain Japan tour packages include public transportation, primarily the subway, as a cost-saving measure. This option is suitable for travelers who are comfortable walking an average of

20,000+ steps per day. For families or retired couples seeking a more hassle-free experience to maximize enjoyment, we highly recommend a private tour with a dedicated vehicle.

Embark on an 11-Day Traditional Japan Tour encompassing Osaka, Hiroshima, Kyoto, and Tokyo, immersing yourself in the rich cultural heritage and captivating beauty of Japan's iconic destinations.

7 TOP PLACES TO VISIT IN JAPAN

Based on our extensive travel experience in Japan, we understand the challenge of selecting from the multitude of incredible destinations this country has to offer. Below, we present some of our preferred locations, curated through our firsthand exploration and meticulous holiday planning in Japan.

1) TOKYO: MODERNITY & JAPANESE ANIME

Tokyo, as a bustling and contemporary capital city, presents an abundance of attractions encompassing culinary delights, expansive shopping malls, revered temples, captivating museums, and awe-inspiring sky bars, along with the iconic Mount Fuji in the backdrop.

Beyond these renowned landmarks, we can curate a range of hand-picked activities to enhance your travel experiences. For instance, immerse yourself in the art of sushi-making at a local home, relish it as a delightful lunch, and delve into the lore of legendary samurai warriors by donning an authentic samurai costume.

Tokyo holds great appeal for those visiting Japan due to the interests of their children, particularly teenagers. With various theme parks such as J World, the Pokemon Center, and Tokyo Disneyland, Tokyo offers an ideal setting to captivate their fascination with anime.

2) KYOTO: ANCIENT TEMPLES & GEISHA

Kyoto boasts a wealth of prominent ancient sites and historical landmarks awaiting exploration. This city presents distinctive and authentic experiences that are not to be missed.

The striking Fushimi Inari Shrine, renowned for its countless vermilion torii gates and featured in the film "Memoirs of a Geisha," stands as a captivating testament to Kyoto's allure. To fully immerse yourself in traditional Japanese accommodation, consider staying at a cozy ryokan with its old-style tatami bedrooms. For an extraordinary culinary experience and an opportunity to witness a geisha en route to a tea house, a visit to Kyoto's Gion district is highly recommended. As you stroll along lantern-lined cobblestone streets, you will be transported back in time, enveloped in the ambiance of a bygone era.

Nature is never far in Kyoto, allowing you to revel in the lush bamboo groves of Arashiyama or indulge in the ethereal beauty of cherry blossoms in numerous renowned locations.

3) HAKONE: RYOKANS & HOT SPRINGS

Hakone, celebrated throughout Japan for its picturesque splendor and natural hot springs, emerges as one of the most sought-after destinations in the country. The Hakone region boasts over a dozen natural hot springs, enveloped by ryokans that offer an idyllic retreat for indulging in delectable kaiseki meals and bathing in the rejuvenating waters.

When not luxuriating in the therapeutic hot springs, take the opportunity to explore the quaint and unspoiled town situated along the shores of Lake Ashinoko, with the majestic Mount Fuji providing a captivating backdrop.

4) NARA: DEER PARK
Nara, an ancient Japanese city conveniently located within an hour's journey from Kyoto and Osaka, entices visitors primarily due to Nara Park, often referred to as Deer Park by locals. This expansive park is home to over a thousand freely roaming deer, providing delightful encounters throughout its grounds and offering the opportunity to feed them in designated areas.

5) TAKAYAMA AND SHIRAKAWA-GO: RURAL COUNTRYSIDE
Takayama, situated in the mountainous Hida region, presents an ideal retreat from the bustling cities, allowing visitors to unwind and relish a few tranquil days in the rural countryside. The city invites exploration of its well-preserved townhouses, savoring the renowned Hida beef, and visiting local sake breweries for a taste of mellow sake.

After immersing oneself in the charms of Takayama, many travelers opt to venture to Shirakawa-go, renowned for its immaculately preserved Old Town. This region showcases traditional gassho-zukuri farmhouses, some of which have withstood the test of time for over 250 years. During the winter months of January and February, these farmhouses are beautifully illuminated at night, creating a captivating wintry ambiance that draws numerous visitors.

Embark on your tailor-made tour planning now. Our dedicated travel consultant will respond within one working day.

6) KANAZAWA: ANCIENT CITY DURING THE EDO PERIOD

Kanazawa, an ancient city in Japan, holds great significance as it was once home to one of the most influential clans in the country during the Edo period. Today, Kanazawa offers a captivating glimpse into Japan's rich ancient culture, making it an excellent destination for enthusiasts seeking to explore the country's historical heritage.

Remarkably, Kanazawa stands as one of the few areas that remained untouched by air raids during World War II, preserving its numerous ancient districts. It is a remarkable opportunity to witness the architectural remnants and atmosphere of a bygone era. Additionally, Kanazawa provides a unique insight into the lives of samurais and geishas, allowing visitors to delve into the intricacies of their lifestyles and traditions.

7) SAPPORO: SNOW SCENERY AND WINTER SPORTS

Sapporo, the capital of Hokkaido province and Japan's fifth-largest city holds a prominent place among winter destinations. Its climatic conditions result in an abundance of snowfall, making it an ideal location for winter sports enthusiasts. Notably, Sapporo hosted the prestigious Winter Olympics in 1972, further solidifying its reputation as a hub for winter activities.

Georgia Tucker

Beyond its captivating winter scenery and a plethora of sporting resorts, Sapporo boasts the renowned annual Snow Festival. This grand event, spanning a week in February, captivates the hearts of more than two million visitors each year. Recognized globally, the festival enthralls attendees with its astonishing ice sculptures, leaving an indelible impression of Sapporo's artistic and cultural vibrancy.

9-Day Best of Japan's Winter - Hokkaido Private Tour100% refund before 3 weeks before departure

How Many Days to Stay In Japan?

For a comprehensive introduction to Japan's highlights, we recommend allocating at least a week to visit the two most prominent cities:

3 days in Tokyo

3 days in Kyoto

1 day in Osaka

To further explore Japan's picturesque destinations, such as Hakone and Takayama, an additional two to three days would be beneficial. We offer meticulously designed itineraries catering to three popular trip lengths: 9, 14, and 17 days. Each itinerary is thoughtfully curated to provide a balance of immersive experiences and leisure time. Furthermore, we can customize the itinerary based on your preferences and allocate free days for relaxation or independent exploration.

Georgia Tucker

CHAPTER TWO

DISCOVERING KYOTO

WELCOME TO KYOTO

Enveloped by mountains and renowned for its Zen gardens, Buddhist temples, historic statues, delightful shopping experiences, and delectable cuisine, Kyoto stands as one of Japan's most enchanting destinations. My delight stemmed from aimlessly wandering through temples, indulging in a variety of gardens, and strolling amidst the captivating bamboo forest. The city's allure attracts a significant influx of visitors, especially during peak seasons. While attempting to explore Kyoto early in the day can mitigate crowds to some extent, it is challenging to entirely avoid them. Therefore, preparation and opting for off-peak periods are advisable. To help plan your visit and navigate around crowds while also maximizing cost savings, this comprehensive Kyoto travel guide serves as a valuable resource.

TOP THINGS TO SEE AND DO IN KYOTO

Georgia Tucker

1. Visit Gion

Gion, renowned as Kyoto's esteemed geisha district, offers an enchanting experience. Take a leisurely walk along the main street to witness the captivating acharyas (geisha tea houses), charming local shops, and myriad restaurants adorning the district. Consider joining a guided walking tour of Gion to delve deeper into the rich history and captivating geisha culture. (Please note that photography is prohibited on the narrow private streets in Gion to ensure the privacy of geishas, as they carry out their daily activities while attracting significant tourist attention.)

2. Check Out Heian Shrine

Heian Shrine, an esteemed Shinto shrine, stands as one of the most cherished and frequented sites in the country. Its entrance is graced by a magnificent torii gate, and the shrine itself boasts a vibrant and intricately adorned exterior that beautifully contrasts with the lush surrounding gardens. While entrance to the shrine is free, a fee of 600 JPY is required to explore the garden.

3. Day Trip To Nara

Nara, recognized as a UNESCO World Heritage Site, captivates visitors with its abundance of "wild" deer roaming freely throughout Nara Park. These deer hold cultural significance as messengers of the gods, and visitors can purchase deer crackers to hand-feed these gentle creatures. Don't miss the opportunity to visit Todai-ji, the world's largest wooden building, which dates back to the 8th century and was meticulously reconstructed in the 1700s. It is important to remain vigilant of personal belongings in the park, as the deer are known to have an appetite for anything within reach, including food, paper maps, and more.

4. Visit Kinkaku-Ji (The Golden Pavilion)

Kinkaku-ji, officially known as Rokuon-ji, is a Zen Buddhist temple that forms an integral part of Kyoto's collective UNESCO World Heritage Site. Although the temple has faced destruction and subsequent reconstructions over the centuries, the current incarnation, dating back to the 1950s, showcases the top two floors adorned entirely in resplendent gold leaf, thus earning its moniker, the Golden Pavilion. As one of the country's most visited destinations, Kinkaku-ji captivates visitors with its timeless allure. Admission to the temple is priced at 400 JPY.

5. Visit Arashiyama (The Bamboo Forest)

For a tranquil escape, immerse yourself in the serene ambiance of Arashiyama's bamboo forest. Stroll along its picturesque trails, allowing the gentle sway of the towering bamboo to envelop your senses. Adjacent to the renowned Tenryu-ji temple, this natural wonder stands as one of Japan's most breathtaking locations. Given its immense popularity, arriving early is advisable to fully relish the beauty of the forest undisturbed by crowds. Entry to Arashiyama is free of charge.

OTHER THINGS TO SEE AND DO IN KYOTO

1. Tour Nijo Castle

Nijo Castle, one of the 17 Historic Monuments of Ancient Kyoto and a UNESCO World Heritage Site, was originally constructed in 1603 for Tokugawa Ieyasu, the first shogun of the Edo Period. Over time, it transformed from an imperial palace to a public landmark. Spanning 170 acres, the castle encompasses tranquil Zen gardens, intricate interior artwork, and a defensive moat. Due to its popularity, it is advisable to arrive early in the morning to avoid crowds. The entrance fee is 800 JPY, with an additional 500 JPY required for entry into Ninomaru Palace, one of the two palaces within the castle. English audio guides, which I highly recommend, are available for 500 JPY.

2. Visit The Kyoto Imperial Palace Park

Kyoto Gyoen, also known as Imperial Palace Park, once served as the residence of the Imperial family and court nobles until 1868 when the capital was relocated to Tokyo. The present-day palace dates back to 1855, and although entry into the buildings is restricted, visitors are free to explore and appreciate the surroundings—an uncommon privilege as guided tours were previously mandatory.

3. Walk Around Higashiyama

Higashiyama, one of the oldest and most well-preserved sections of Kyoto, offers an enchanting experience. Dedicate an afternoon to exploring the historic streets and neighborhoods on the east side of the Kamo River. The narrow streets are adorned with quaint shops showcasing local specialties such as Kiyomizu-yaki pottery, okashi (candy), pickled foods, handicrafts, and other regional souvenirs.

4. Visit Ryoan-Ji Temple

Among the temples I visited in Kyoto, Ryoan-ji Temple stood out as my favorite. Constructed in the 15th century, this UNESCO World Heritage Site houses a mausoleum containing the remains of seven emperors from Japan's history. The meticulously maintained traditional rock and sand garden, regarded as one of the finest in the country, serves as a captivating representation of Buddhist art and philosophy. Admission is priced at 500 JPY per person.

5. Wander Among The Plum Blossoms

If your visit to Kyoto falls between mid-February and mid-March, you'll have the opportunity to witness the blooming of plum blossoms. Similar to Japan's renowned cherry blossoms, the plum trees burst forth with vibrant white and dark pink flowers. Two notable locations to admire these blossoms are Kitano Tenmangu and the Kyoto Botanical Gardens, both situated in northern Kyoto. Admission to Kitano Tenmangu shrine is free (except for the Plum Grove, which incurs a fee of 1,000 JPY), while entrance to the botanical gardens is priced at 200 JPY.

6. Explore The Kyoto National Museum

Established in 1897, the Kyoto National Museum houses an extensive collection of artifacts, ceramics, and fine art. Renowned as one of Japan's top-rated museums, it boasts over 12,000 items, with a focus on pre-modern Japanese and Asian art. The admission fee is 700 JPY for the permanent exhibit, 1,600-1,800 JPY for temporary collections, and 300 JPY for access to the museum gardens.

7. Kyoto International Manga Museum

Catering to both manga enthusiasts and art aficionados, the Kyoto International Manga Museum is home to an extensive collection of over 300,000 manga. Established in 2006, the museum features various exhibits highlighting the evolution of manga art over the years, along with workshops conducted by manga artists. Visitors can also peruse vintage antique manga dating back to the 1860s and 1880s. Admission to the museum is priced at 900 JPY.

8. Relax In An Onsen

Kyoto boasts over 140 bathhouses, known as onsens, preserving a tradition that traces its roots back to the early Middle Ages. Segregated by gender, these bathhouses offer a wonderful opportunity to unwind and immerse oneself in the unique aspects of Japanese culture. It's important to note that some onsens prohibit visitors with tattoos or require them to be covered, so it's advisable to check beforehand. Budget bathhouses typically charge around 1,000 JPY. Among the city's options, Tenzan-no-yu Onsen stands out as a premier choice.

9. Eat At Nishiki Market

Nishiki Ichiba, an enclosed market, offers an exceptional array of locally grown fruits, vegetables, and fresh seafood, showcasing the vibrant flavors of the region. While visiting, indulge in yuba, a delectable delicacy derived from the "skin" formed on the surface of soymilk vats. When dried, it becomes irresistibly crispy and delightful, although you may also savor it in the form of soymilk doughnuts and ice cream. Located on Nishikikoji Street, the market's operating hours vary by shop but typically span from 9 am to 6 pm. To delve deeper into Japanese gastronomy, consider embarking on a food tour of the market, which includes tantalizing tastings at Nishiki, as well as matcha and desserts in the nearby Gion district.

10. Go Hiking

The picturesque hills surrounding Kyoto provide an idyllic setting for hiking enthusiasts. Scattered throughout these hills are numerous Buddhist temples and religious sites, including serene Zen gardens. Mount Atago, situated nearby, offers a moderate 4-6-hour hike that rewards participants with awe-inspiring views of the city and its verdant surroundings, while also presenting opportunities to encounter abundant wildlife, including the graceful deer that inhabit the area. For those seeking a lengthier hiking adventure, the Takao to Hozukyo trail provides a moderately challenging trek spanning just over 6 hours.

11. Experience A Tea Ceremony

Tea holds a significant position within Japanese culture, and the traditional Japanese tea ceremony originated in Kyoto during the 16th century as a means for elites to impress one another. To this day, Kyoto remains the epicenter of tea culture in Japan and offers the ideal setting to acquaint oneself with this unique art form. Immerse yourself in the tranquility of a tea ceremony, either within one of the city's temples or through a workshop led by a seasoned tea master, where you can acquire the skills to perform the ceremony yourself.

12. Take A Cooking Class

With Japanese cuisine's global reputation, why not enhance your culinary repertoire by partaking in a cooking class? Kyoto presents various options, ranging from immersive sessions in izakayas, and casual bars/restaurants, to acquiring the skills to craft your bento boxes.

KYOTO TRAVEL COSTS AND BUDGET

Hostel Prices - In Kyoto, most hostels charge between 2,400-3,500 JPY per night for dormitory rooms of various sizes. For those seeking privacy, private rooms with twin or double beds typically range from 7,500-10,000 JPY per night. These prices remain relatively consistent throughout the year. Complimentary Wi-Fi and lockers are standard amenities, and self-catering facilities are available in many hostels for guests who prefer to prepare their meals. However, breakfast is not included in the hostel rates.

Budget Hotel Prices - Budget-conscious travelers can find accommodations in two-star hotels starting at approximately 4,000-6,000 JPY per night for a double bed. Alternatively, capsule hotels offer a unique and compact experience with rates beginning at 2,500-2,800 JPY per night, providing guests with a cozy pod-like space. Though simple, these establishments provide an authentic and distinctly Japanese lodging experience.

Airbnb - Due to stringent regulations, securing Airbnb accommodations in Japan, including Kyoto, can be challenging. Listings are often located outside the city center, and prices tend to be higher. Private apartments or homes listed on Airbnb generally start at around 10,000-20,000 JPY per night. For a single room, prices typically begin at a minimum of 7,500 JPY.

Food - Japanese cuisine's reputation precedes it, and it has earned a coveted spot on UNESCO's Intangible Heritage List. Wherever you are in Japan, rice, noodles, seafood, and fresh seasonal produce prominently feature in the culinary landscape. Kyoto, renowned for its Buddhist monasteries and vegetarian cuisine, specializes in tofu, while the region also excels in the production of tea, including matcha, an experience best savored through a traditional tea ceremony. Mochi candy, made from pounded rice and often filled with sweetened bean paste, provides a delightful treat. Basic food options such as curry and donburi (meat and rice bowls) typically cost around 500-700 JPY, while ramen is usually priced below 1,200 JPY. Fast-food establishments like McDonald's or KFC offer basic combo meals for around 750 JPY. For a more economical culinary experience, explore the local street food scene, where green tea sweets and sashimi sticks are available for approximately 300 JPY, and Japanese pancakes offer a filling option for only 200 JPY. Convenient stores like 7-Eleven also provide affordable options, with pre-set meals of noodles, rice balls, tofu, and pre-packaged sushi available for under 500 JPY, making them a popular choice among locals. Supermarkets also offer similar set meals at comparable prices.

Mid-Range Restaurants - For a more extensive dining experience encompassing three-course meals, expect to pay around 2,500-3,000 JPY per person.

Kaiseki Ryori - Originating in Kyoto, Kaiseki Ryori represents an elevated style of Japanese dining. This high-end culinary experience comprises a multi-course meal, typically featuring seven courses encompassing a range of dishes, from chicken to sushi. Prices for a Kaiseki Ryori set menu start at around 8,000-10,000 JPY. For a more indulgent option, a wagyu steak course, accompanied by rice, seafood, salad, dessert, and more, begins at 10,000 JPY.

Beverages - Domestic beer is priced at approximately 450-550 JPY, while sake, a traditional Japanese alcoholic beverage, usually costs around 800 JPY per glass. A latte or cappuccino is typically 500-600 JPY, and a bottle of water is approximately 150 JPY.

Groceries - Basic staples such as rice, vegetables, and fish can be purchased for approximately 4,000-5,500 JPY per week. It is advisable to thoroughly wash all produce, as agricultural practices in Japan often rely on peak productivity and employ pesticides due to limited arable land.

Backpacking Kyoto Suggested Budgets

When backpacking in Kyoto, it is recommended to budget around 7,000 JPY per day. This budget assumes staying in a hostel dormitory, preparing most meals, dining at affordable 100 yen shops, limiting alcohol consumption, visiting free museums and temples, and utilizing public transportation for getting around.

For a more moderate budget of 16,000 JPY per day, you can opt for a private hostel or Airbnb room, dine out for most meals, enjoy some drinks, visit additional paid attractions, occasionally use taxis, and have more flexibility in your travel arrangements.

On a "luxury" budget, anticipate spending 26,000 JPY per day or more. This budget allows for accommodation in a mid-range hotel, dining at nice restaurants, indulging in more drinks, participating in paid tours such as food tours or cooking classes, and overall enjoying a more comfortable trip. However, this luxury budget serves as a starting point, and the possibilities are endless!

The chart below provides an overview of the estimated daily budget for different travel styles. It's important to note that these figures represent average daily costs, and actual expenses may vary from day to day (with the potential to spend less each day). The aim is to provide a general idea for budget planning. All prices are in JPY.

Accommodation

Food

Transportation

Attractions

AVERAGE DAILY COST

Backpacker

2,500

2,000

1,500

1,000

7,000

Mid-Range

7,000

5,000

2,000

2,000

16,000

Luxury

10,000

8,000

4,000

4,000

26,000

MONEY-SAVING TIPS

While the aforementioned prices may appear substantial, there are several ways to reduce costs and save money during your visit to Kyoto. Here are some quick tips to help you stay within your budget:

1. **The Subway & Bus One-Day Pass**

Consider purchasing this card if you plan to use public transportation extensively. One-day passes for adults cost 1,100

JPY (550 JPY for children) and provide unlimited travel on both the subway and city buses.

2. The Traffica Kyoto Card

This prepaid card offers a 10% discount on public transportation (bus and subway) within the city. You can load it with 1,000 or 3,000 JPY, but note that unused funds cannot be refunded, so only acquire the card if you anticipate using the full amount.

3. Shop at the 100 Yen stores

Kyoto has numerous 100 Yen shops offering set meals, groceries, beverages, toiletries, and household items. Inquire at your hotel or hostel reception for the nearest "Hyaku En" shop.

4. Eat at 7-Eleven

7-Eleven, Family Mart and other convenience stores in Kyoto offer a variety of affordable pre-packaged meals, including sandwiches, soups, fruit, and traditional Japanese options, making them a budget-friendly choice for lunch. Supermarkets also provide similarly priced set meals.

5. Cook your food

Most hostels in Kyoto provide kitchen facilities where you can prepare your meals, significantly reducing food expenses.

Combine this with shopping at 100 Yen stores for even greater savings.

6. Eat curry, ramen, and donburi

These three dishes—curry, ramen, and donburi—offer inexpensive and satisfying meal options in Kyoto's dining scene. Embracing these choices allows for affordable dining-out experiences.

7. Work for your room

Many hostels in Japan offer the opportunity to work in the morning, typically cleaning, in exchange for free accommodation. This arrangement can be an excellent way to save money, especially if you plan to stay in one area for an extended period.

8. STay with a local

Hospitality platforms like Couchsurfing enable you to stay with locals, providing not only free accommodation but also the chance to engage with residents and gain insights into local life. However, it's advisable to send your requests early, as response times can be slow. Expats can also be more active on the platform, so consider reaching out to them as well.

By implementing these money-saving tips, you can optimize your budget while enjoying your time in Kyoto.

9. **Buy food at night**

Many supermarkets in Kyoto offer significant discounts on fresh and prepared food after 8 pm, as they aim to sell their remaining stock. By taking advantage of these evening deals, you can save up to 50% on a wide range of fresh food items.

10. **Get a JR Pass**

If you plan on traveling to Kyoto by train and intend to visit other cities as well, consider purchasing a Japan Rail Pass. This pass provides unlimited train travel and can lead to substantial cost savings. Available in 7, 14, and 21-day options, it is important to note that the pass can only be obtained outside of Japan, so it is advisable to plan ahead accordingly.

11. **Rent a bicycle**

Kyoto offers numerous rental options for bicycles, including many hostels and rental companies. Renting a bike is a cost-effective and convenient way to explore the city, providing a more immersive experience. Standard bicycles typically range from 800-1,000 JPY per day, while e-bikes are available for approximately 1,700-2,000 JPY per day.

12. **Bring a water bottle**

The tap water in Kyoto is safe to drink, making it advisable to bring a reusable water bottle. By doing so, you not only save money but also contribute to reducing plastic waste. Lifestraw offers reusable bottles with built-in filters, ensuring clean and safe drinking water throughout your journey.

WHERE TO STAY IN KYOTO

Kyoto boasts a variety of comfortable and sociable hostels. The following recommendations are highly regarded accommodations in the city:

- Backpackers Hostel K's House Kyoto
- Len Kyoto
- Kyoto Hana Hostel
- Gojo Guest House
- Gion Ryokan Q-beh

HOW TO GET AROUND KYOTO

Public Transportation - Getting around Kyoto is effortless with its extensive bus network operated by multiple companies. The buses are reliable and clean, and offer single-fare tickets starting at 230 JPY, with prices increasing based on the distance, traveled. Exact change is required when disembarking, obtainable from the machine near the driver at the front of the bus.

Kyoto also features a metro system consisting of two lines and over 30 stations. Single fares vary depending on the distance traveled and generally range from 210-350 JPY per person.

If you anticipate frequent use of public transportation, it may be beneficial to acquire one of the reloadable cards available in the city. The Traffica Kyoto Card, a prepaid card, offers a 10% discount on bus and subway fares within Kyoto. It can be loaded with 1,000 or 3,000 JPY (unspent funds cannot be refunded). Alternatively, a one-day pass priced at 1,100 JPY is valid for both buses and subways.

Taxi - While taxis are readily available in Kyoto, they can be relatively expensive. Starting rates are typically 600 JPY, with an additional 465 JPY per kilometer traveled. Utilizing public transportation is advised whenever possible.

Ridesharing - Didi serves as the primary ridesharing app in Kyoto (Uber is also available), but prices are generally comparable to taxis, offering limited savings.

Bicycle - Kyoto is a bicycle-friendly city, and renting a bike provides an enjoyable and convenient means of transportation. Standard bikes can be rented for approximately 800-1,000 JPY per day, with e-bikes available for around 1,700-2,000 JPY per day. It is recommended to reserve a bike in advance or arrive early, especially during the summer months. Additionally, please note that traffic in Kyoto follows a left-hand driving pattern.

Car Rental - International Driving Permit (IDP) holders can rent cars in Kyoto; however, it is often unnecessary. Car rentals typically cost around 7,500 JPY per day. It is important to remember that driving in Japan involves left-hand traffic, and obtaining an IDP before arriving in the country is necessary. Unless there is a specific requirement for a car, relying on public transportation and trains, which are generally faster, is recommended.

For competitive car rental prices, consider using Discover Cars.

Train - If your travel plans include visiting other cities in Japan, including nearby Nara accessible in under an hour, consider purchasing a Japan Rail Pass. These passes, available for 1, 2, or 3 weeks, offer free travel on all JR lines and can result in significant savings, particularly for those embarking on an extensive itinerary.

WHEN TO GO TO KYOTO

The peak season to visit Kyoto is during the summer, but this period can be uncomfortably hot, with temperatures exceeding 32°C (89°F) and high humidity from June to August. September also remains warm. Furthermore, larger crowds are expected as Kyoto is one of Japan's most popular destinations, particularly due to the fame of its bamboo forest on social media platforms. To mitigate the effects of the heat and crowds, it is advisable to rise early to avoid congestion and secure accommodation reservations well in advance.

The shoulder seasons, April-May and October-November, are optimal times to visit Kyoto. During these periods, temperatures are milder, and rainfall is generally limited. However, note that late March to early April marks cherry blossom season, resulting in significant crowds. If planning to visit during this time, make sure to make arrangements in advance.

While winters in Kyoto are chilly, the temperatures remain bearable. Daytime temperatures average around 10°C (50°F), dropping to approximately 1°C (34°F) at night. The city is relatively tranquil during this season. Snowfall is common, but it tends to melt shortly after. Rainfall is also frequent, so dressing appropriately for wet and brisk weather is recommended.

Moreover, be aware that typhoon season occurs between May and October. Japan is well-prepared to handle typhoons; however, it is advisable to purchase travel insurance in advance as a precautionary measure.

Georgia Tucker

HOW TO STAY SAFE IN KYOTO

Japan is widely recognized as a remarkably safe country, including the city of Kyoto, where the likelihood of encountering robbery, scams, or harm is virtually nonexistent. Nonetheless, it is advisable to maintain a vigilant mindset and securely safeguard your valuables as a precautionary measure.

Solo female travelers, in general, can feel secure in Kyoto; however, adhering to standard precautions remains essential. These precautions encompass never leaving drinks unattended at bars and avoiding walking alone while intoxicated, among others. It is worth noting that sporadic instances of lewd behavior, such as unsolicited personal inquiries or catcalling, have been reported by some female travelers, although these occurrences are infrequent.

When traveling outside the city, it is worth considering that most train companies now designate "women-only" cars during rush hours. Clear signage in pink directs female passengers where to board. While scams are rare in Kyoto, if concerns persist about potential fraudulent activities, it is advisable to familiarize yourself with common travel scams to avoid.

The primary risk to be mindful of in Kyoto stems from natural events. Earthquakes and typhoons are common occurrences, and it is important to acquaint yourself with emergency exits upon arrival at your accommodation. Additionally, downloading offline maps to your phone can prove invaluable for navigating the city during emergencies.

In the event of an emergency, Japan's emergency number is 110, or you can seek assistance by calling the Japan Helpline at 0570-000-911. Purchasing comprehensive travel insurance is undoubtedly the most crucial advice. Travel insurance offers protection against illnesses, injuries, theft, and trip cancellations, providing comprehensive coverage in case any unforeseen circumstances arise. I never embark on a trip without travel insurance, as I have found it indispensable on numerous occasions.

ACCOMMODATION IN JAPAN - RYOKAN

Stay in Ryokan in Japan
While Japan offers a wide range of accommodation options, our preferred choice is the Ryokan. A ryokan is a traditional Japanese inn that provides a unique blend of comfort and relaxation. These establishments typically feature floors made of rice or bamboo straw, and guests sleep on traditional mattresses placed directly on the floor. Additionally, ryokans offer delightful kaiseki-style dinners made with fresh ingredients.

Ryokans epitomize comfort, with their staff often dressed in kimonos and providing excellent service. The cuisine served is of top-tier quality, and many ryokans are situated near natural hot springs, known for their therapeutic properties. The ryokans in Hakone, renowned for their hot springs, are particularly famous, offering a blend of Japanese and Western-style rooms and an ambiance of tranquillity and harmony.

Georgia Tucker

Georgia Tucker

Georgia Tucker

CHAPTER THREE

GREAT ITINARY IDEAS

JAPAN IN 14 DAYS: TRAVEL ITINERARY

For those embarking on their first trip to Japan, a two-week itinerary allows for a comprehensive exploration of the country's highlights. Here is an optimal 14-day itinerary covering Tokyo, Kyoto, Osaka, Hiroshima, Fukuoka, and more.

Day 1: First Taste Of Tokyo
Sensoji Temple - Harajuku - Shibuya Crossing

Commence your 14-day journey with a visit to the vibrant and spiritually significant Sensoji Temple, located in Asakusa. Explore the adjacent bustling streets, brimming with local delicacies and captivating shops.

Ensure you don't miss the eccentric and diverse neighborhood of Harajuku, renowned for its fashion-forward subcultures. Immerse yourself in the vibrant shopping scene and witness the dynamic evolution of Japanese culture, from historical temples to Harajuku's unique fashion district.

Lastly, make your way to Shibuya Crossing, Tokyo's iconic landmark. Located in the heart of the city, this bustling intersection offers an immersive experience of Japanese culture and provides a glimpse of modern Tokyo at its finest.

Day 2: Relaxing Tokyo
Yanaka – Gyokurin-ji – Yanaka Cemetery

• Embark on a stroll through the captivating district of Yanaka, a rare haven in Tokyo where the essence of old-world charm, traditional Japanese lifestyle, and serenity have gracefully endured the test of time. Of particular interest within this area is Yanaka Ginza Street, a delightful haven for feline enthusiasts as it boasts shops brimming with the presence of these charming creatures.

• Discover Gyokurin-ji, a hidden gem nestled in the Yanaka district. This serene temple is home to an ancient chinquapin tree, adding to its tranquil ambiance.

• Pay a visit to Yanaka Cemetery, an unexpectedly peaceful place that draws the curiosity of many. Here, you will find the eternal resting place of the renowned Tokugawa Yoshinobu, the last of the Shoguns from the Edo Period.

Day 3: Final Day In Tokyo
Ryogoku Kokugikan – Robot Restaurant – Tokyo Skytree

• If your visit aligns with a sumo tournament, do not miss the opportunity to witness these captivating events. Ryogoku Kokugikan stands as one of the finest arenas worldwide to witness the art of classical sumo wrestling, making it an unforgettable experience for first-time spectators.

• Immerse yourself in the extraordinary atmosphere of the Robot Restaurant (located at the Shinjuku stop on the Yamanote line).

Indulge in the ultimate encounter of being served by gigantic robots controlled by bikini-clad girls. This one-of-a-kind experience has captivated international tourists, leaving them yearning for more.

- Conclude your exploration of Tokyo with a grand finale at the Tokyo Skytree, offering breathtaking vistas of the city during the day and a magical spectacle at night. As the second tallest structure globally (after the Burj Khalifa in Dubai), it provides a captivating panorama.

Day 4: Wonderful Kyoto
Higashiyama District, Kodaiji Temple, and Maruyama Park

• Commence your Kyoto adventure with a visit to the enchanting Higashiyama District. This historically significant locale exudes an authentic Kyoto ambiance and has been impeccably preserved throughout the centuries. Between the Yasaka Shrine and the Kiyomizudera Temple, narrow streets and wooden shops transport visitors to a bygone era, showcasing the essence of Japan's former capital.

• Explore the Kodaiji Temple, located within the same area, and uncover its hidden secret—the serene bamboo grove nestled behind its grounds. A stroll through this bamboo forest offers a truly unique and timeless experience.

- Delight in the beauty of Maruyama Park, renowned for its abundant cherry trees. This picturesque park has become a popular destination for both tourists and locals during the enchanting cherry blossom season (late March to early April).

Day 5: Classic Kyoto
Saiho-ji, Funaoka Onsen, and Okitsu Club

Kyoto, once the imperial capital of Japan for over a millennium, continues to captivate both residents and newcomers alike. On day 5, we recommend exploring the following highlights:

- Visit the Saiho-ji temple, home to one of Japan's most exquisite gardens. Designed in 1339, these heart-shaped gardens offer a breathtaking view and an authentic atmosphere that embodies ancient Japanese traditions.

- Indulge in a truly ancient experience at Funaoka Onsen, a remarkably preserved establishment offering a range of saunas, indoor and outdoor baths, electric baths, stone-lined outdoor bathing areas, and herbal baths. Allow yourself to indulge in the abundant pleasures and relaxation available here. For a complete experience, we recommend a visit to the nearby Tahitchi restaurant, where a warming bowl of miso soup awaits.

- Immerse yourself in Japanese culture by visiting the Okitsu Club Kyoto. This esteemed organization provides a comprehensive introduction to the roots of traditional Japanese culture, allowing visitors to immerse themselves in the elegance and delicacy that define ancient Japanese traditions.

Day 6: Final Day In Kyoto
Nishiki Market, Fushimi Inari, and Nanzen-ji

• Delight in the culinary delights of Nishiki Market, a vibrant hub offering fresh seafood, traditional Japanese cooking techniques, and affordable prices. Conveniently located just a 3-minute walk from Shijo Station, Karasuma, or Kawaramachi Station, this market is the perfect place to savor the local cuisine.

• Explore the majestic Fushimi Inari-Taisha shrine, renowned for its iconic appearance in numerous movies. The vibrant torii gates and serene atmosphere make it a must-see destination for travelers from around the world.

• Conclude your Kyoto journey at Nanzen-ji, a grand temple that has played a significant role throughout centuries. Regarded as the "First Temple of the Land" and one of the five great Zen temples of Kyoto, it has been an integral part of Kyoto's landscape since 1291. The awe-inspiring view it offers captures the essence of its grandeur and power.

Day 7: Nara Day Trip
Todai-ji, Nara-Koen Park, and Nara National Museum

• Todai-ji: Renowned as one of Nara's most iconic temples, Todai-ji houses the imposing Daibutsu, also known as the Great Buddha. Standing at an impressive height of 14.98 meters and weighing 500 tons, this temple preserves a significant collection of national treasures while serving as a revered site for traditional Buddhist rituals. Visitors from across Japan journey here to pay homage to the deities and offer their prayers.

- Nara-Koen Park: A splendid oasis of natural beauty, Nara-Koen Park seamlessly merges history, tranquility, and the delightful presence of wild deer. While these animals may approach in search of food, they pose no harm. However, once fed, they may follow visitors with persistent curiosity.

- Nara National Museum: This institution provides a comprehensive insight into the history and distinctions between the two types of Buddhist statues. The museum boasts both permanent and temporary exhibitions, showcasing exquisite sculptures, painted art, and calligraphy.

Day 8: Amazing Osaka

- Lifestyle Museum of Osaka: Situated in a ten-story edifice, this museum offers visitors a glimpse into Osaka's ambiance during the 1830s. Step into a typical street adorned with shops, pharmacies, and ancient public baths. Through artful lighting, the museum recreates the daytime and nighttime atmospheres of the Edo period, immersing guests in a captivating experience.

- Osaka-jo (Osaka Castle): Originally constructed in 1583 under the direction of General Toyotomi Hideyoshi, Osaka Castle stands as a testament to his power. Spanning lush grounds, the castle encompasses tea houses, secondary citadels, impressive gates, and over 600 cherry trees, creating a picturesque scene.

- Osaka Aquarium Kaiyukan: Esteemed as one of the world's largest and most remarkable aquariums, Osaka Aquarium Kaiyukan offers an enriching experience. We highly recommend a visit, particularly for those traveling with children.

Day 9: Final Day In Osaka

• Umeda Sky Building: A truly iconic structure, Umeda Sky Building boasts 40 stories and twin towers that converge in the middle. Offering a panoramic 360-degree view of Osaka from lofty heights, the building's magnificence is particularly striking at night.

• Dotonbori: Among Osaka's most popular and essential tourist destinations, Dotonbori encompasses an entire city within a single street. This vibrant locale abounds with charming boutiques, intriguing shops, and captivating tourist attractions.

• Kuromon Ichiba Market: Established in 1920, this expansive indoor market is located a short 10-minute walk from Dotonbori, making it an ideal destination after a stroll. Kuromon Ichiba Market offers an abundance of fresh seafood, vegetables, and meat, providing an excellent opportunity for a satisfying meal after a day of exploration.

Day 10: The History Of Hiroshima

• Hiroshima Peace Memorial Park: A testament to the resilience and the pursuit of peace, this memorial park aims to inspire the world even after enduring profound suffering. Surrounded by serene green spaces and clear waters, the park exudes tranquility. The A-Bomb Dome, symbolizing the city's commitment to peace, stands as a striking reminder of the past.

• Hiroshima Castle: Visible from various points in the city, Hiroshima Castle offers a glimpse into the era of samurai. Ascend the hill and climb the stairs to discover the breathtaking sight of the castle, where you will be transported back in time.

- Mitaki-dera Temple: Tucked away, Mitaki-dera Temple remains a hidden gem of Hiroshima. Enveloped by the natural beauty of its surroundings, the temple takes its name from the three waterfalls within its grounds. This peaceful sanctuary showcases the innate allure of nature.

Day 11: Miyajima Day Trip

- Miyajima: Referred to as Shrine Island, Miyajima is a renowned and picturesque destination. Just a short ferry ride from the coast of Hiroshima (accessible with your Japan Rail Pass), this enchanting island offers breathtaking views throughout the day and into the night.

The Great Torii at Itsukushima (Miyajima)

- Itsukushima Shrine: A marvel of Japanese architecture, Itsukushima Shrine captivates visitors with its ethereal beauty. The highlight of this sacred site is the Torii gate, seemingly floating in the radiant blue waters. A serene boat ride offers a timeless experience, immersing guests in the elegance of Japanese craftsmanship.

- Momijidani Park: Stroll through this verdant wonderland and revel in its tranquility. For a quieter experience, opt for the smaller trail indicated by signs rather than the direct route leading to Mt. Misen. Soon, you will find yourself amidst magnificent forests, adorned with towering trees that offer shelter during rainy days and a refreshing breeze in the summer heat.

Day 12: Surprising Fukuoka

Fukuoka, often overlooked by many travelers, offers a delightful surprise as a perfect final destination for your trip to Japan. Its notable attractions include:

• Ohori Park – Originally a castle moat, this meticulously designed park resembles a magnificent water garden centered around a picturesque pond.

• Fukuoka Castle Ruins (Maizuru Park) – Unveiling the remnants of a colossal 17th-century castle, this area invites visitors to explore its historical significance and immerse themselves in the past.

• Gokoku Shrine – Situated close to Fukuoka Castle, Gokoku Shrine stands as the heart of Fukuoka's vibrant modern life. Engaging in Japanese rituals, festivals, and celebrations, this captivating shrine leaves a lasting impression regardless of the season.

Day 13: Final Day In Fukuoka

• Tocho Ji Temple – An ancient temple boasting remarkable antiquity, Tocho Ji safeguards a 30-ton Buddha statue and a collection of rare artifacts amassed throughout its rich history.

• Kawabata Shotengai – Serving as one of the city's oldest streets, Kawabata Shotengai exudes a nostalgic ambiance. As you stroll along this charming thoroughfare, you'll feel transported back in time, captivated by its unique shopping allure.

• Fukuoka Tower – Concluding your visit, we recommend an illuminated panoramic view of Fukuoka from atop Fukuoka

Tower. As a popular rendezvous spot for couples, the tower features a designated area called Lover's Sanctuary, where lovers can have their names or initials engraved on padlocks.

Day 14: Return To Tokyo

On the final day, relax and enjoy the journey back to Tokyo aboard the bullet train. Sit back and savor the memories of your remarkable trip.

Note: Utilize your Japan Rail Pass for a complimentary ride on the Narita Express. Remember to make seat reservations before boarding.

Day 15: Other Destinations

For additional information on other enticing destinations such as Nikko, Kamakura, Takayama, Kanazawa, Hakone, or Mount Fuji, we invite you to explore further possibilities for your future travels.

THE ULTIMATE JAPAN ITINERARY FOR FIRST-TIMERS: FROM 1 TO 3 WEEKS

It is rare to encounter a traveler who did not fall in love with Japan. The country's appeal lies in its exquisite cuisine, rich history and culture, breathtaking landscapes, and the genuine warmth and politeness of its people.

Georgia Tucker

Japan remains one of my favorite destinations, always leaving me yearning for more, no matter the duration of my stay. As Japan reopens its doors to travelers, there is a rush to experience its wonders. Even those who have longed to visit for years are now embarking on their inaugural journey. However, the country may still appear somewhat daunting to some, harboring a perception of exoticism that might discourage exploration.

Where should you go? What should you see? How can you make the most of your time? Fortunately, with Japan's compact size and efficient high-speed trains, it is remarkably easy to traverse vast distances and experience a multitude of destinations in a short period.

To assist you in planning, I have curated suggested itineraries based on my extensive visits, offering a balance between renowned landmarks and off-the-beaten-path experiences that embody the true essence of Japanese culture.

JAPAN ITINERARY: ONE WEEK

Day 1 & 2: Tokyo

Commencing your journey in Tokyo, the vibrant capital city and home to the country's major international airport is a common starting point. If your trip spans seven days, it is advisable to activate your JR Pass upon arrival, enabling you to avail yourself of the complimentary JR trains that traverse the city.

While Tokyo offers a plethora of captivating attractions that can easily occupy your entire week, here are some noteworthy highlights:

• Explore Toyosu Fish Market: As the world's largest fish market, Toyosu plays a crucial role in the global sushi supply chain. Witness the exhilarating daily auctions, which are instrumental in sustaining this culinary tradition. While entry is free, guided food and drink tours of the Tsukiji Outer Market are available at an approximate cost of 13,500 JPY.

• Visit Sensoji Temple: Adorned with exquisite paintings, Sensoji Temple occupies a picturesque location near a striking five-story pagoda and the renowned Kaminari Gate. Inside the main hall resides a magnificent statue of Kannon, the goddess of mercy. Despite the bustling crowds, this temple is a sight that should not be missed.

• Experience the charm of Golden Gai: The narrow alleys of Golden Gai are home to a multitude of atmospheric bars, creating a lively ambiance reminiscent of a red-light district. Whether you indulge in libations or simply take a stroll, this unique destination is not to be overlooked.

• Discover the Imperial Palace: While entry into the 15th-century imperial residence is restricted, the surrounding palace grounds offer a serene setting for a leisurely walk. Immerse yourself in the tranquility of this historic site.

• Witness a Sumo Match: If your visit coincides with a sumo wrestling tournament, it is highly recommended to witness this iconic cultural spectacle. Due to high demand, securing tickets in advance, approximately priced at 3,800 JPY, is advisable.

For those with additional time, consider taking a day trip to Kamakura to marvel at the colossal Daibutsu (Great Buddha). Standing at a remarkable height of over 13 meters (42 feet), this ancient statue dates back to the 13th century. The journey to Kamakura takes approximately 90 minutes each way, and the cost is covered by the JR Pass.

To indulge in delectable cuisine, I suggest visiting Uogashi Nihon-Ichi (Standing Sushi Bar), Nemuro Hanamaru KITTE Marunouchi, Motodane, Tokyo Whisky Library, Ichiran Shibuya, and Uohama, as they offer an array of culinary delights.

Days 3 & 4: Kyoto

Kyoto, widely regarded as Japan's most captivating city, evokes a sense of stepping back in time. Nestled amidst picturesque mountains and adorned with temples, gardens, and bamboo forests, Kyoto exudes a unique charm. It is advisable to plan your visit outside the peak summer season to avoid excessive crowds. Nevertheless, the city offers an array of remarkable attractions:

• Discover the Golden Pavilion: This iconic temple, also known as Kinkaku-ji, dates back to the 1950s when it was reconstructed after a fire. The temple, a UNESCO World Heritage Site, attracts countless visitors due to its stunning beauty and historical significance.

• Explore Gion: Renowned as the historic geisha district, Gion enthralls visitors with its traditional charm. Wander along the main street, observe acharyas (teahouses where geishas entertain), explore the quaint shops, and savor the culinary delights offered by the district's numerous restaurants. A guided walking tour of Gion is available for approximately 1,600 JPY.

• Experience the Bamboo Forest: Escape to Arashiyama and immerse yourself in the tranquil ambiance of the bamboo forest. Located near the renowned Tenryu-ji Temple, this ethereal setting offers a serene respite from the bustling city. Arriving early allows for a more peaceful experience, devoid of large crowds.

• Admire Ryoan-ji Temple: Ryoan-ji Temple, my personal favorite in Kyoto, showcases a splendid rock and sand garden and houses a mausoleum containing the remains of seven emperors. Designated as a UNESCO World Heritage Site, this temple boasts one of the country's finest gardens.

For a half-day excursion, consider visiting Nara, a small city located just an hour from Kyoto. Nara served as Japan's capital in the eighth century, resulting in a wealth of ancient buildings and temples that have withstood the test of time. One of the city's main attractions is the sacred deer, which freely roam the area. Offering them crackers or observing their carefree presence is a memorable experience. Don't miss the opportunity to visit Todai-ji, the world's largest wooden building, housing a majestic 16-meter (52-foot) Buddha statue. Todai-ji is also recognized as a UNESCO World Heritage Site, and admission costs 500 JPY.

Day 5: Osaka

As Japan's third-largest city and a financial hub, Osaka's culinary delights steal the spotlight. Indulge in mouth-watering sushi, sashimi, Kobe beef, Japanese BBQ, flavorful ramen, as well as local specialties like okonomiyaki (savory pancake with egg and vegetables) and kushikatsu (skewered kebabs). Embark on a food tour priced at approximately 12,000 JPY or savor the culinary delights while leisurely exploring the city.

While exploring Osaka, make sure not to miss Osaka Castle. Although the current version dates to 1931, it remains an impressive architectural marvel. The castle premises house a small yet enlightening museum and an observation deck offering picturesque city views. Additionally, a stroll along Dotonbori, the city's main street, is highly recommended, especially in the evening when the vibrant atmosphere, lined with numerous restaurants, stores, and dazzling neon lights, creates a captivating experience.

Day 6: Hiroshima

On August 6, 1945, Hiroshima endured the catastrophic impact of the first-ever deployment of a nuclear weapon on a populated area, an event that caused immense devastation. The atomic bomb unleashed by Allied forces claimed the lives of over 80,000 individuals and resulted in a firestorm that ravaged the city, leaving 70% of it in ruins. Moreover, approximately 70,000 people suffered injuries in the aftermath.

Presently, Hiroshima has successfully revitalized itself. A visit to the Atomic Bomb Museum is essential, as it offers a poignant portrayal of the city's history before and after the pivotal event. Through photographs, artifacts, videos, and information on the impact of radiation, the museum provides a somber and thought-provoking experience that should not be overlooked.

If you desire a change of scenery, consider venturing to Miyajima, an island renowned for its natural beauty and hiking trails. A cable car ride to the mountain summit rewards visitors with breathtaking vistas. The ferry journey to Miyajima, lasting a mere 10 minutes, is complimentary for holders of the JR Pass.

Day 7: Tokyo
Return to Tokyo for your departure flight. With a journey of just under four hours on the bullet train, you will have ample time to further explore before bidding farewell.

JAPAN ITINERARY: TWO WEEKS
If you have allocated 14 days for your Japan adventure and have obtained a rail pass, the following division of time is recommended:

DAYS 1-9
Follow the aforementioned itinerary, allocating an additional day in Tokyo and, depending on your interests, including either Osaka or Kyoto.

Day 10: Takayama
Takayama, a charming small city, boasts a captivating historic district known as Sanmachi Suji, dating back to the Edo Period (1603–1868). Its narrow streets are lined with traditional wooden structures, evoking a nostalgic ambiance that transports visitors to a bygone era. Teahouses, cafés, and sake breweries are among the notable establishments. For an immersive experience of Japan's past, do not miss the opportunity to visit Hida Minzoku Mura Folk Village, which showcases a collection of traditional thatch-roof houses.

Takayama is renowned for its Hida beef, a variety known for its high-fat content and exquisite taste, surpassing even the renowned A5 Wagyu. Indulging in this delicacy is a must while in the city. Additionally, for hiking enthusiasts looking to prolong their stay in the region, the Japanese Alps are in proximity. A visit to Kamikochi offers the opportunity for a day hike or an overnight excursion, with trails of varying difficulty levels available from April to November. Hakusan National Park, reachable within an hour by car, also features hiking trails.

Day 11: Kanazawa

Often referred to as "Little Kyoto," Kanazawa boasts an impeccably preserved Edo-era district. Here, you can admire numerous historic samurai residences, including the restored Nomura House, open for public viewing. The Ninja (Myoryuji) Temple stands out as one of Japan's unique temples, constructed as a defensive structure in defiance of strict regulations prohibiting local lords from fortifying their domains. The temple conceals hidden rooms, secret tunnels, and a labyrinth of staircases and corridors designed to perplex potential adversaries.

For a break from urban exploration, a mere hour south of Kanazawa lies Hakusan National Park, home to Mount Haku, one of Japan's revered holy mountains.

Day 12: Matsumoto

Set against breathtaking scenery, Matsumoto is home to one of the nation's best-preserved castles, Matsumoto-jo (Matsumoto Castle), which dates back to 1594. While certain sections have undergone reconstruction, the main structure remains authentic. Its distinct black exterior has earned it the moniker "Crow Castle." Visitors fortunate enough to be present in April can witness the awe-inspiring displays of cherry blossoms for which the region is renowned. Furthermore, similar to Takayama, Matsumoto is near the Japanese Alps, offering access to exceptional hiking opportunities.

Days 13 & 14: Hakone

Situated a mere 100 kilometers (62 miles) from Tokyo, Hakone is a captivating region celebrated for its natural hot springs or onsen. Nestled within a national park, this picturesque area offers breathtaking vistas of Mount Fuji and Lake Ashinoko, making it an ideal destination for a serene and rejuvenating retreat.

A wide selection of hotels, both contemporary and traditional in style, provides guests with the opportunity to indulge in their private hot springs, both indoor and outdoor. These soothing waters afford visitors a chance to unwind while immersing themselves in the surrounding beauty.

While embracing relaxation and tranquility, be sure to embark on a cable car ride to ascend the mountain and revel in even more awe-inspiring panoramas. The region is encompassed by craters resulting from an inactive volcano eruption approximately 80,000 years ago (distinct from the nearby active volcano, Mount Fuji). At the summit, numerous vendors offer eggs cooked in sulfurous waters, as the folklore suggests that consuming them extends one's lifespan by seven years—an intriguing opportunity to explore local customs and traditions.

For those inclined towards a hiking adventure, a trail leading up the mountain is accessible between July and September. The duration of the trek, ranging from 5 to 12 hours, varies depending on one's fitness level. Many hikers opt to commence their ascent during the night, ensuring arrival at the summit by daybreak. Along the way, small shops provide sustenance, and advanced reservations for rented beds are available for those desiring to divide their journey. It is essential to conduct thorough research and adequately prepare, as this hike poses a significant physical challenge.

For a more tourist-oriented experience, consider taking a leisurely ride on a mock pirate ship that navigates the enchanting lake, granting further opportunities to appreciate the majestic mountains, including the iconic Mount Fuji.

Full-day tours encompassing Hakone's key attractions are available for 14,000 JPY.

JAPAN ITINERARY: THREE WEEKS

If you have the luxury of an additional week in Japan, allocating more time to each destination enables a more unhurried exploration of the country's wonders.

Drawing from the aforementioned suggestions, here is an itinerary that optimizes your time:

- Days 1-3: Tokyo
- Day 4: Mount Fuji or Hakone
- Day 5: Takayama
- Days 6 & 7: Kanazawa
- Days 8 & 9: Matsumoto

- Days 10-12: Kyoto

- Days 13 & 14: Osaka

- Days 15 & 16: Hiroshima

Day 17: Train To Hokkaido

Embarking on a train journey to Hokkaido, Japan's northernmost island renowned for its volcanic landscapes and rugged terrain, entails a travel time of approximately 15-16 hours. Sleeper cars are available, albeit with an additional surcharge of around 9,500 JPY to secure a bed. If desired, one can disembark at Hakodate for a brief respite and to stretch their legs. Alternatively, travelers can proceed directly to Sapporo, Hokkaido's capital, with an additional train journey of approximately three hours.

For those opting to spend a few hours in Hakodate, a visit to the Morning Market is highly recommended. This bustling market offers an abundance of fresh seafood for culinary enthusiasts to savor. Additionally, exploring Fort Goryokaku, the first fort in Japan built in a "Western" style, provides insight into the country's history.

Alternatively, to minimize travel time, a two-hour flight from Hiroshima to Sapporo is available at an approximate cost of 12,000 JPY for a one-way ticket.

Days 18-20: Sapporo

Sapporo, the fifth-largest city in Japan, stands apart from the rest of the country, offering a distinctive cultural experience. Originally inhabited by the indigenous Ainu people, the region witnessed a substantial increase in Japanese immigration during the 19th century, resulting in a flourishing Japanese population.

While in Sapporo, a visit to the local Beer Museum, owned by Sapporo Breweries, the oldest beer company in the nation, is highly recommended. This captivating establishment showcases the history of beer in Japan and traces the brewery's origins. Whiskey aficionados will also delight in The Bow Bar, renowned for its collection of rare and exquisite whiskeys, establishing it as one of the premier whiskey bars globally.

Sapporo's geographical location is particularly noteworthy, as the region boasts some of the finest hiking opportunities in the country. With its abundance of hills and mountains, visitors can engage in both day hikes and overnight excursions. Noteworthy peaks include Mount Me-akan, Mount Asahim, Mount Mashu, and Nishibetsu-dake. To capture the most breathtaking views of the city, ascend Mount Moiwayama via a 30-60-minute hike or by taking the convenient cable car.

During the winter months, Sapporo becomes a haven for snow sports enthusiasts, boasting over a hundred ski resorts. Equipment rentals for skiing or snowboarding are available at prices ranging from 4,500 to 10,000 JPY, while lift passes typically cost between 4,000 and 6,000 JPY per day. Don't miss the annual Sapporo Snow Festival held every February, drawing over two million visitors. The festival features stunning ice sculptures, igloos, live music performances, and a delectable array of local cuisine.

Additionally, a day trip to Otaru is highly recommended, where visitors can indulge in the freshest uni (sea urchin) available in the entire country. Exploring the markets, stalls, and shops in the area provides an opportunity to satisfy culinary cravings and relish Hokkaido's renowned seafood delicacies.

Day 21: Home!
It is now time to make your way back to Tokyo or consider taking the overnight train from Sapporo. As your journey draws to a close, savor these final hours in Japan and immerse yourself in the experiences that await.

Japan offers an abundance of captivating sights and activities, and even with the duration of your trip, it is merely a glimpse of what this remarkable country has to offer (we haven't even touched upon Okinawa and the islands!). While these itineraries may seem fast-paced, it's important to note that Japan is not known for being an inexpensive destination. Budget-conscious travelers often find it necessary to maintain a swift pace to manage expenses effectively.

Regardless of the length of your visit, Japan guarantees an awe-inspiring, breathtaking, and distinctive experience that never fails to captivate. While it may not be as affordable as its neighboring countries, the time and investment you put into exploring Japan will undoubtedly be rewarding. Prepare to be amazed!

1) 9-Day Classic Route: Major Highlights Of Japan And A Ryokan Experience

Immerse yourself in Japan's iconic attractions and indulge in a traditional ryokan experience on this classic 9-day itinerary:

Here is a hand-picked itinerary of classics for you to consider:

Days 1–3: Tokyo (sushi-making, discover samurai, Meiji Shrine, anime, and Disneyland)

Days 4–5: Hakone (stay at a ryokan with an onsen)

Days 6–8: Kyoto (geishas, Fushimi Inari Shrine, sample sake, and Kaiseki, and feed deer in Nara)

Day 9: Osaka (Dotonbori district and Osaka Castle)

Tokyo - Hakone - Kyoto - Osaka

This itinerary encompasses the essence of Japan, including visits to the historic Asakusa district in Tokyo, the samurai museum, iconic landmarks like the Meiji Shrine, anime-themed experiences, and the enchantment of Disneyland. Additionally, you will have the opportunity to unwind in a traditional ryokan with an onsen in Hakone and savor Osaka's vibrant street food scene.

RECOMMENDED ITINERARY

9-Day Japan Highlights TourTokyo - Hakone - Kyoto - Osaka

2) 14-DAY PRIVATE FAMILY ROUTE: LEARNING THROUGH FUN

Embark on a 14-day journey that combines education and entertainment, providing enriching experiences for the whole family:

Tokyo - Takayama - Hiroshima - Kyoto

This itinerary encompasses visits to major attractions in Japan's cities, allowing for a blend of educational and enjoyable activities. Marvel at the panoramic views from Tokyo Tower, explore a traditional folk village in Takayama, pay homage to peace at Hiroshima Peace Memorial Park, experience the tranquility of a cozy ryokan, stroll through the enchanting bamboo groves of Kyoto, and create lasting memories at Universal Studios in Osaka.

Here Is The Summary Itinerary For You:

Days 1–3: Tokyo (Visit Meiji Shrine, Tsukiji Market, Pokemon Center, and Akihabara)

Days 4–5: Takayama (Explore Hida Folk Village, sample sake and Hida beef)

Days 6–7: Hiroshima and Miyajima (Visit Peace Memorial Park and the iconic 'Floating Torii Gate')

Days 8–11: Kyoto (Experience geisha culture, stay in a ryokan, visit Nijo Castle, feed deer in Nara, and wander through the enchanting bamboo groves in Arashiyama)

Days 12–14: Osaka (Discover the Cup Noodle Museum, Super Nintendo World, and Universal Studios)

Get your family to the heart of Japan's beauty.

2-Week Japan Private Family Vacation: Discover the diversity of Japan with your kids.

3) 17-Day Japan Itinerary: Hands-On Experiences And Outdoor Activities

Tokyo – Kamakura – Kawaguchiko – Karuizawa – Nagoya – Kyoto – Osaka

To create an unforgettable journey through Japan, you and your family or partner can embark on a marvelous trip that includes the following experiences: immerse yourself in a samurai experience and the Edo vibe of Asakusa in Tokyo, enjoy a light hike surrounded by nature in Karuizawa, have fun at the lovely Ghibli Park or the technologically-rich Nagoya City Science Museum in Nagoya, savor a memorable geisha dinner and experience a cozy night at a ryokan in Kyoto, and explore the remarkable Osaka Castle while indulging in the excitement of Universal Studios in Osaka.

HERE IS THE ITINERARY FOR YOUR INSPIRATION:

Days 1–4: Tokyo (Visit Meiji Shrine, try sushi-making, engage in a ninja experience, explore samurai culture, and ascend Tokyo Tower)

Day 5: Kamakura (Discover the giant bronze Buddha and Hasedera Temple)

Day 6: Lake Kawaguchi (Marvel at Mount Fuji and enjoy biking)

Days 7–8: Karuizawa (Explore the national park and embark on a light hiking adventure)

Days 9–11: Nagoya (Experience the wonders of Ghibli Park and visit the Toyota Commemorative Museum of Industry and Technology)

Days 12–14: Kyoto (Engage with geisha culture, stay in a ryokan, visit Kinkakuji Temple, explore Arashiyama, and feed deer in Nara)

Days 15–17: Osaka (Discover the Cup Noodle Museum, explore Osaka Castle, and indulge in the excitement of Universal Studios and Super Nintendo World theme park)

Georgia Tucker

HOW TO BUDGET AND SAVE MONEY TIPS

Japan has garnered a reputation for being an expensive travel destination, but this perception does not align with the reality on the ground. With thoughtful planning and strategic choices, your visit to Japan can be budget-friendly and cost-effective. Many of the country's prominent attractions, for instance, do not require an admission fee, and free festivals occur throughout the year. By employing the following invaluable tips, you can stretch your yen further and derive maximum value from your journey through Japan.

Consider Staying in A Business Hotel

Business hotels offer economical accommodations with private rooms and en suite facilities. It is possible to find double rooms for as low as ¥8000 (and single rooms for as low as ¥6000), although prices may be slightly higher in cities such as Tokyo, Kyoto, and Osaka. Seek out options that include a complimentary breakfast buffet, as these can provide substantial sustenance for an extended period.

Book Direct at A Guesthouse Or Hostel

Japan boasts an array of excellent guesthouses and hostels throughout the country. Not only are these establishments typically clean and well-maintained, but they often feature English-speaking staff who provide service akin to a concierge. The cost of a double or single room is comparable to that of a business hotel, although shared facilities are more common. Dormitory beds can be secured for approximately ¥3000 (US$23). Some accommodations may charge extra for towel rentals, so consider bringing your own. Additionally, booking directly with the establishment may result in slightly lower rates compared to using third-party booking sites.

Sleep In a Capsule Hotel In The Cities

Capsule hotels offer compact rooms that consist of a bed, providing a cost-effective solution for overnight stays. While the price of a capsule berth is slightly higher than a dormitory bed in a hostel (around ¥4000 per night), the added privacy is worth considering. While it may not be desirable to stay exclusively in capsule hotels, they can serve as a budget-saving option in cities where traditional hotels tend to be more expensive.

Go Camping in The Summer Months

For those seeking an affordable option to experience Japan, the country's network of well-maintained campsites in rural or resort areas is a reliable choice. Prices for camping range from ¥500 to ¥1000 per person or tent. Note that many campsites operate only during the summer months.

The Japan Rail Pass Is a Great Travel Bargain

Similar to the renowned Eurail Pass, the Japan Rail Pass offers exceptional value for travelers on a budget. This pass allows unlimited travel on Japan's extensive rail network, including the renowned shinkansen (bullet train). The JR Pass is available for purchase online or through travel agents such as JTB in your home country. It's worth noting that there are region-specific train passes that offer reduced rates, so carefully evaluate your itinerary before making a decision.

Ride Local Trains for Less With The Seishun 18 Ticket

The Seishun 18 Ticket provides a cost-effective option for local train travel, subject to specific conditions. Priced at ¥12,050 (US$100), this ticket grants five one-day passes that are valid for travel on regular Japan Railways trains, excluding the Shinkansen and high-speed limited express trains. The ticket has a limited usage period, is typically available during school holidays, and can only be purchased from JR ticket windows in Japan. If the timing aligns and you prefer a leisurely pace of travel, this unique and economical option allows for convenient exploration within Japan.

Swap A Night in A Hotel For An Overnight Bus Ride

Long-distance buses, particularly those operated by Willer Express, offer a budget-friendly means of transportation, with the added benefit of overnight routes that can save a night's cost in accommodation. Additionally, bus passes are available, further enhancing the affordability of this option.

Consider Renting a Car To Go Beyond The Cities

While highway tolls and petrol prices in Japan can be costly, renting a car can be a cost-effective choice, especially for group or family travel or when venturing away from major rail hubs.

This option allows for greater flexibility in exploring regions beyond the cities.

Take Domestic Flights with Low-Cost Airlines
Japan features several low-cost airlines, such as Peach, Jetstar, and Air Do, offering competitive pricing for domestic flights. When considering this option, it is important to factor in the additional time and cost associated with airport transportation.

Japan's Shrines and Temples Are Free To Visit
The majority of Shintō shrines in Japan do not require an admission fee for entry, while many temples allow visitors to tour the grounds without charge, reserving fees for specific areas such as halls or walled gardens. This provides an opportunity to experience Japanese religious and cultural heritage at no cost.

Eat Cheap Food and Meet Locals At A Traditional Festival
Throughout the year, festivals held at shrines, temples, and city streets offer a free and engaging way to witness the vibrancy of traditional Japanese culture. These events often feature affordable food vendors, providing an excellent chance to savor local cuisine while interacting with the community.

Opt For Hikes and Walking Tours
Engaging in hikes or walking tours presents a cost-free and enriching experience during your trip. Explore emerging city neighborhoods, traverse ancient pilgrimage trails or rural

pathways, or venture into the mountains within Japan's national parks. For architecture enthusiasts, planning a self-guided tour to admire renowned buildings designed by prominent Japanese architects is also possible with assistance from tourist information centers or accommodations.

Spend Time Relaxing in The City Parks

Urban parks, typically free to enter, along with some gardens, attract locals on weekends and provide a serene setting for activities such as picnicking and people-watching. Visitors with impeccable timing may even witness the captivating beauty of Japan's cherry blossoms in bloom.

Shop For Cheaper Goods at A Local Market

Seaside towns, rural areas, and traditional open-air markets in certain cities offer opportunities to immerse in local culture while finding reasonably priced, fresh produce. Exploring these markets provides a unique window into the community and facilitates affordable shopping experiences.

Choose The Right Dish in The Right Place To Save Money

Dining at shokudō, comparable to casual eateries, allows you to enjoy a satisfying meal for under ¥1000 (US$7.50). Many establishments offer delicious ramen at prices as low as ¥600 (US$5), while tachigui, stand-and-eat counters, serve soba and udon noodles starting from ¥350 per bowl. Upscale restaurants often provide discounted lunchtime courses, enabling patrons to relish a substantial meal at significantly lower prices than during dinner hours. Moreover, it is customary in Japan to receive complimentary tea and water at restaurants, and tipping is not expected.

Bentō Are a Budget Alternative To A Meal Out

These pre-packaged meals, consisting of a variety of dishes, can be purchased for less than ¥1000 at supermarkets. For a slightly higher price, department store food halls offer gourmet bentō, which can often be purchased at a discounted price shortly before closing.

Get Everything You Need and More At The Convenience Store

Convenience stores are a boon for budget-conscious travelers. They stock a range of items such as sandwiches, rice balls, hot dishes, and even beverages, allowing you to assemble an affordable meal (although not necessarily a healthy one). Most accommodations provide kettles, making cup noodles a convenient option.

A GUIDE TO DAILY COSTS IN JAPAN

Capsule hotel room: ¥4000 (US$30)

Standard double room: ¥8000 (US$60)

Self-catering apartment (including Airbnb): ¥6000 (US$45)

Georgia Tucker

Coffee: ¥400 (US$3.50)

Sandwich: ¥300 (US$2.20)

Pint of beer at a bar: ¥600 (US$4.50)

Dinner for two: ¥5000 (US$38)

Two-person karaoke session for an hour: ¥2000 (US$15)

22 WONDERFUL THINGS TO DO IN JAPAN

WHAT TO DO FOR FUN IN JAPAN

Curating a list of the finest experiences in Japan is no easy task, given the abundance of captivating and enjoyable activities this country offers.

While every island in Japan holds its allure, the cities of Osaka, Kyoto, and Tokyo stand out for hosting numerous must-see attractions, making them ideal for first-time visitors.

Japan's cultural offerings encompass a remarkable range of old and new treasures. You can board a futuristic bullet train, explore ancient temples, or visit a samurai castle, all in a single day. Despite having visited Japan multiple times over the years, our fascination with this country remains unwavering. It consistently ranks among our favorite travel destinations worldwide.

Continue reading for a selection of our top recommendations on how to make the most of your time in Japan!

Georgia Tucker

1. Visit The Samurai Castles

Japan preserves numerous castles from its medieval era when samurai warriors reigned supreme. These fortresses exemplify artistic mastery and provide captivating explorations. While several samurai castles are scattered throughout the country, two standout options are Himeji Castle (near Osaka and Kyoto) and Matsumoto Castle (near Tokyo). This experience undoubtedly ranks among the best and is budget-friendly.

2. Wear A Kimono

Japan boasts an abundance of kimono rental shops, allowing you to immerse yourself in the country's iconic traditional attire for a day. Renting a kimono in Tokyo and capturing memorable photos at the renowned Shibuya Crossing was a highlight for my wife and me. Kyoto, with its numerous temples and shrines, also offers fantastic photo opportunities. It's worth noting that locals are not offended by foreigners embracing the kimono; in fact, they appreciate others enjoying their culture.

3. Stroll A Landscape Garden

Japanese gardens are renowned for their immaculate beauty and photogenic charm. Throughout Japan, you'll find a plethora of these gardens, perfect for strolls and relaxation. While these gardens are delightful year-round, they truly shine during the fall season when vibrant foliage colors emerge, typically in November. Exploring these gardens is one of our cherished activities in Japan.

4. Join A Tea Ceremony

Immersing oneself in the rich cultural tradition of Japan, a Japanese tea ceremony offers a captivating experience. This revered ceremonial practice takes place on a tatami mat, with meticulous preparations preceding its commencement. Delicately infused with artistic nuances, the tea ceremony embodies values of purity, tranquility, respect, and harmony, cherished by the Japanese people. Even for those not particularly inclined towards tea, this ceremonial encounter provides a valuable glimpse into Japanese culture and history. Some venues may also offer the option to rent a kimono, elevating the experience to a more immersive and distinctive level.

5. Ride A Bullet Train

Embarking on a train journey is always a delight, and Japan boasts some of the world's most exceptional train systems.

Renowned for their efficiency, these trains traverse awe-inspiring scenic routes, particularly in rural areas. Among these remarkable trains, the futuristic shinkansen, commonly known as the bullet train, hold a special allure. Capable of reaching speeds of several hundred kilometers per hour, riding the shinkansen becomes an exhilarating experience. These high-speed trains can be accessed in prominent cities such as Kyoto, Osaka, and Tokyo.

Travelers can also opt for the Japan Rail Pass, also referred to as the JR Pass, which offers unlimited rides on JR trains for one, two, or three weeks. This cost-effective pass presents an excellent opportunity for long-distance train travel throughout Japan.

6. See The Landmarks

The three major cities of Osaka, Kyoto, and Tokyo host a plethora of renowned landmarks that epitomize the essence of Japan. Among the standout sights are the enchanting Arashiyama

Bamboo Grove in Kyoto, the majestic Todaiji Temple in Nara, and the colossal Kamakura Buddha in Tokyo. It is also worthwhile to venture beyond urban areas to witness natural landmarks like Mount Fuji and Lake Kawaguchi, both feasible options for immersive day trips from Tokyo.

7. Visit The Temples & Shrines

Japan's landscape is adorned with ancient temples and shrines, each possessing its own captivating allure and photographic appeal. While Kyoto boasts an array of notable temples, every region in Japan showcases unique temple designs and rich historical backgrounds. Must-visit recommendations include the revered Sensoji Temple in Tokyo, the resplendent Kinkakuji Temple in Kyoto, and the captivating Fushimi Inari Shrine, also located in Kyoto.

8. See The Koyo (Fall Colors)

Japan's autumn season is a visual spectacle, as vibrant hues of orange, red, pink, and yellow paint the foliage. The optimal time to witness the captivating fall colors, known as "koyo," varies depending on the destination. However, in Kyoto and Tokyo, the foliage generally reaches its peak in the middle to late November. These vivid displays of nature's beauty offer an unforgettable experience that lingers in one's memory.

9. See The Sakura (Cherry Blossoms)

The Sakura season, characterized by the enchanting bloom of cherry blossoms, holds enduring popularity in Japan. These picturesque blossoms adorn numerous iconic sights across the country, including Himeji Castle and Mount Fuji. The precise timing of the cherry blossom season varies each year and depends on the region. However, the optimal viewing period typically falls in the last week of March. Experiencing this ephemeral spectacle is an essential activity for visitors to Japan.

10. Feed the Deer At Nara Park

Nara Deer Park offers a remarkable encounter with numerous amiable deer, eager to be fed and photographed. These semi-wild deer roam freely within the sprawling 1,600-acre park, fostering an interactive and joyful experience for visitors. Additionally, the park features a cluster of ancient temples and shrines, remnants of Nara's bygone era as the ancient capital of Japan. Easily accessible as a day trip from Osaka or Kyoto, Nara Park stands out as one of the finest attractions in Japan.

11. Meet the Japanese Snow Monkeys

A highly recommended winter excursion from Tokyo entails visiting Snow Monkey Park near Nagano. While it is feasible to undertake this as a day trip, it is preferable to allocate two days for a more relaxed experience. Immerse yourself in the company of Japanese macaques as they indulge in the natural hot springs amidst the mountainous surroundings. Observing their playful antics provides endless amusement, offering ample opportunities for capturing memorable photographs. The journey involves a moderate level of hiking, but the breathtaking snowy vistas along the way add to the allure of this excursion.

12. See Mount Fuji

As Japan's tallest peak and an iconic symbol of the country, Mount Fuji captures the imagination. You will encounter this majestic mountain on postcards, souvenirs, and artistic representations throughout Japan, making it essential to witness its splendor firsthand. The Fuji Five Lakes region presents a remarkable day trip option from Tokyo. The picturesque lakes and the Chureito Pagoda, an exquisite five-story red pagoda set against the backdrop of Mount Fuji, offer prime photography opportunities. Although Mount Fuji was once an active volcano, it has remained dormant for centuries, with its last eruption dating back to 1707. For hiking enthusiasts, ascending Mount Fuji is an option. The trail caters to beginners while providing a satisfying workout.

13. Go Up the Tokyo Skytree

Completed in 2012, the Tokyo Skytree stands as the tallest structure in Japan and the world's tallest tower. Soaring to a height of 634 meters (2,080 feet), it currently ranks as the third tallest structure globally, surpassed only by Malaysia's Merdeka 118 and Dubai's Burj Khalifa. A visit to the observation decks via the Skytree's elevators rewards visitors with breathtaking panoramic views of Tokyo from an elevated vantage point. The more adventurous can venture onto a section featuring a glass floor, offering a captivating view straight down. The Tokyo Skytree welcomes visitors throughout the year, operating from 10 AM to 9 PM. A nighttime visit is particularly captivating, allowing for a glimpse of Tokyo's illuminated cityscape. Undoubtedly, the Tokyo Skytree ranks among the top attractions in Japan.

14. Shop for Souvenirs

No visit to Japan would be complete without exploring the realm of souvenir shopping. Beyond the customary fridge magnets and keychains, you can discover unique treasures such as art paper fans, ceramic bowls, kimonos, or exquisite Japanese knives. While the Shinjuku and Shibuya districts in Tokyo are renowned shopping havens, unexpected treasures can also be found in unexpected places, such as the street stalls near Sensoji Temple.

15. Enjoy Japanese Food

Where does one even begin? Japan's gastronomy is renowned worldwide, and the culinary delights alone provide ample reason to visit this captivating country. Indulge in the flavors of ramen, sushi, udon, yakitori, and all the other delectable dishes for which Japan is renowned. Even the offerings at convenience stores like 7-Eleven exhibit exceptional quality. In essence, relishing the culinary wonders of Japan stands among the top experiences in the country. While Osaka claims the mantle as Japan's premier food city, destinations such as Tokyo and Kobe have also achieved international acclaim for their gastronomic offerings. Tokyo, in particular, boasts the highest number of Michelin-starred restaurants in the world, exceeding 200 establishments.

16. Try Japanese Snacks

Japanese confectionery presents an intriguing counterpart to its culinary delights. Treats such as Mochi and Daifuku may initially seem unfamiliar, but their unique flavors gradually captivate the palate. Additionally, there is a range of delightful sweet snacks to savor, including Pocky and Melon Pan, as well as innovative interpretations of Western favorites like Kit Kat.

Kit Kat holds a particular fascination in Japan, with the country offering over 300 distinct flavors, including peach, cheesecake, sake, and matcha (green tea). Should one develop an affinity for Japanese snacks, online subscription services such as TokyoTreat provide the opportunity to receive a monthly assortment of exclusive Japanese treats conveniently delivered to your doorstep.

17. Wander Dotonbori Street

The vibrant Dotonbori district stands as a prominent tourism hub in Osaka, particularly enchanting during the evening hours. This lively locale boasts an array of enticing restaurants, food stalls, bars, cafes, and captivating sights. Immersing oneself in the vibrant atmosphere of Dotonbori ranks among the top experiences in Japan, and its abundant culinary offerings make it a true haven for food enthusiasts.

18. See the Famous Shibuya Crossing

The Shibuya Crossing in Tokyo holds international acclaim as the world's busiest pedestrian intersection, accommodating an astonishing flow of up to 3,000 individuals at a time. Observing the spectacle of masses seamlessly traversing the streets, especially during weekends, proves to be a captivating experience. This bustling area also offers excellent shopping and dining options, making it an ideal destination for leisurely exploration.

While at Shibuya Crossing, be sure not to miss the Hachiko dog statue, which serves as a poignant tribute to the unwavering loyalty of a faithful dog. The statue commemorates the touching story of Hachiko, who dutifully awaited his owner, Professor Ueno, at the train station every day, even after his owner's passing. The faithful dog continued this routine for nine years until his demise, eventually being interred alongside his beloved owner in 1935. For a bird's-eye view of the Shibuya Crossing and its surroundings, a visit to the nearby Hikarie skyscraper offers the opportunity to ascend to the 16th-floor lobby and enjoy a panoramic vista of the city.

19. Stay in A Traditional Ryokan

Immerse yourself in the authentic ambiance of a traditional Japanese inn, known as a ryokan, characterized by tatami floor mats, sliding doors, and futon beds laid directly on the floor. The elegant design is often complemented by an exceptional Japanese breakfast and the indulgence of onsen hot springs.

Ryokans have been an integral part of Japanese culture since ancient times, with their origins tracing back to as early as 700 AD. However, in metropolitan areas, modern-style hotels have largely replaced them. While Tokyo still offers some exquisite ryokan-style accommodations, it is worth noting that they tend to be pricier and less plentiful. For a more immersive ryokan experience, Kyoto and other regions of Japan often provide a wider range of options.

20. Take A Cooking Class

Embarking in a Japanese cooking class presents an enjoyable opportunity to learn the art of preparing typical Japanese dishes, including sushi, tempura, teriyaki chicken, and miso soup. Platforms such as GetYourGuide offer a variety of highly-rated cooking classes, with Tokyo and Kyoto serving as particularly popular locations. Typically spanning around three hours, these classes not only provide hands-on cooking instruction but also offer insights into the cultural background and significance of each dish.

Participants can opt for a private class guided by a local chef or join a group session, which often offers a more cost-effective option. All necessary ingredients, along with aprons and utensils, are provided, and after the cooking class, participants have the pleasure of savoring the Japanese meal they have skillfully prepared.

21. Visit The Samurai Museum

Experience the essence of Japan's rich history by visiting the renowned Samurai Museum in Tokyo. This captivating attraction is a must-see during your Japan trip, as it showcases an impressive collection of swords, armor, helmets, guns, and various other artifacts of historical significance.

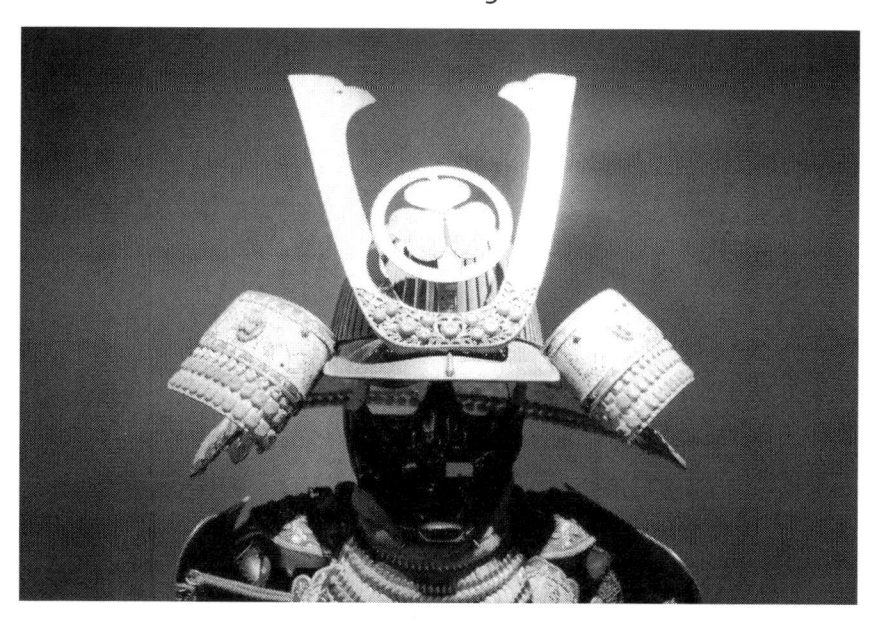

While the entrance fee may be slightly higher, it grants you access to a complimentary guided tour conducted in English, providing valuable insights into the exhibits. The displays are truly remarkable, offering a fascinating glimpse into the world of the samurai. As a memorable highlight, visitors have the opportunity to have their photograph taken while adorned with a traditional Samurai helmet, and for those seeking an immersive experience, the option to don a complete Samurai costume is also available.

Regrettably, due to the ongoing impact of the COVID-19 pandemic on travel, the museum has been temporarily closed. However, we hope that the museum will reopen shortly, allowing visitors to once again immerse themselves in the captivating world of the samurai. No visit to Japan would be complete without a trip to the Samurai Museum in Tokyo. The museum showcases a fascinating collection of swords, armor, helmets, firearms, and other historical artifacts. While the entrance fee may be higher compared to other attractions, it includes a complimentary guided tour conducted in English, enhancing the educational experience. After the tour, visitors have the opportunity to don a Samurai helmet for a memorable photo or even don a complete Samurai costume for an immersive encounter with Japanese warrior culture.

Please note that due to the impact of the COVID-19 pandemic on travel, the museum has temporarily closed its doors. However, we hope that the museum will reopen soon, allowing visitors to once again explore its captivating exhibits.

22. Try Saké

Saké, a well-regarded Japanese alcoholic beverage derived from fermented rice with an alcohol content of approximately 15 percent, has gained popularity and can be found in bars and restaurants across the Japanese archipelago. Engaging in saké tasting can be an enjoyable venture, particularly in the Kyoto region, where GetYourGuide offers a selection of highly rated activities. These experiences often provide opportunities to sample various saké styles while delving into the drink's historical and cultural significance. Additionally, Japan boasts numerous historic saké breweries, offering the chance to tour these establishments and gain insight into the meticulous process involved in crafting this esteemed Japanese libation.

Georgia Tucker

CHAPTER FOUR

DISCOVERING TOKYO

WELCOME TO TOKYO

Tokyo, the capital of Japan, stands as the world's largest city, with an urban population exceeding 38.5 million residents. Serving as one of Japan's 47 prefectures, it occupies a prominent position within the Kanto region on the southeastern side of Honshu, the country's main island.

Originally a modest fishing village known as Edo, Tokyo transformed into a significant political center and castle town during the 17th century. In 1868, Emperor Meiji relocated the imperial seat from Kyoto to Edo, renaming the city Tokyo, meaning "Eastern Capital."

Today, Tokyo holds a prominent position as a financial, technological, and cultural powerhouse. Embracing global leadership in arts, media, fashion, and entertainment, it boasts an impressive array of exceptional museums, temples, and gardens. Furthermore, its extensive rail network facilitates convenient day trips to neighboring prefectures.

Undoubtedly, one of Tokyo's highlights lies in its culinary offerings. Renowned for its delectable dishes such as sushi, ramen, and monjayaki, the city has emerged as the unrivaled standard-bearer for gastronomy, boasting more than double the number of Michelin Stars found in its closest competitor, Paris. Some even argue that Tokyo surpasses Italy in its mastery of pizza, claiming the world's finest exemplar can be found within its bounds.

THINGS TO DO IN TOKYO

1. Get a Drink at Omoide Yokocho or Golden Gai

In Tokyo, we had the pleasure of exploring two captivating "micro-neighborhoods" known as Omoide Yokocho and Golden Gai, both situated within Shinjuku. These vibrant enclaves consist of a collection of quaint restaurants and izakayas, offering a unique and memorable dining experience.

While Omoide Yokocho, colloquially referred to as "Piss Alley," holds historical significance stemming from the era when public restrooms were absent, its current iteration showcases vast improvements in facilities. Located just outside Shinjuku Station, Omoide Yokocho is a bustling hub brimming with cozy izakayas serving a variety of delectable bar food, including yakitori, ramen, and nikomi.

For an enhanced exploration of Omoide Yokocho, guided tours are available through the byFood platform. A mere 10-minute walk from Omoide Yokocho lies Golden Gai, an equally captivating network of narrow alleyways, comprising over 200 charming bars and restaurants. Characterized by two-story structures, this area provides a glimpse into Tokyo's past, evoking nostalgia and charm.

According to our knowledgeable food tour guide, Golden Gai remains a cherished rendezvous spot for Tokyo's creative individuals, including artists, photographers, film directors, and writers. With its distinctive ambiance, Golden Gai offers a delightful setting to unwind and savor a beverage of choice. Visit Get Your Guide for a curated list of tours featuring Golden Gai.

2. Go on a Food or Bar Hopping Tour

One of our favorite activities is partaking in food or bar hopping tours, as they often lead us to hidden local gems that might otherwise go unnoticed. While thorough research can be fruitful, the expertise of local guides proves invaluable when seeking out the most obscure and remarkable establishments.

During our time in Tokyo, we embarked on an enjoyable Shinjuku food tour with Magical-Trip. Led by our knowledgeable guide, Nori, we had the opportunity to visit three distinct restaurants and explore notable landmarks such as Omoide Yokocho and Golden Gai.

For a visual and informative account of our experience on the Shinjuku Tokyo food tour, please refer to my article. Should this pique your interest, byFood or Magical-Trip offer a range of Tokyo food and bar hopping tours for you to consider.

3. Rent a Kimono

Donning a traditional kimono while exploring Tokyo has become a popular and enriching way to immerse oneself in the city's culture, all while capturing stunning photographs. Although we experienced this in Kyoto, the vibrant streets of Tokyo offer an equally picturesque backdrop. To rent a kimono and enhance your Instagram feed, Klook provides convenient options for such experiences.

4. Go to a Maid Cafe

A distinct and captivating concept, Maid Cafes have gained popularity in Tokyo. These unique establishments fall under the category of cosplay restaurants, where waitresses dress in maid costumes and assume the role of servitude while treating cafe patrons as masters and mistresses.

Although Maid Cafes can be found across various parts of Tokyo and Japan, their concentration remains particularly high in Akihabara, the birthplace of this trend. For recommendations on the finest Maid Cafes in Akihabara, please consult the referenced article. Klook offers vouchers for Maidreamin, the first Maid Cafe mentioned in the list.

5. Take a Cooking Class

Exploring hidden culinary gems through food tours is undoubtedly delightful, but if you desire a deeper understanding of a particular cuisine, enrolling in a cooking class becomes an invaluable experience. It allows you to delve into the intricacies and nuances of the cuisine, akin to peering beneath its culinary hood.

During my stay in Tokyo, I had the pleasure of participating in a captivating cooking class, where I acquired the skills to prepare classic Japanese dishes like udon, tempura, and tamagoyaki. Platforms such as Cookly or byFood offer an extensive selection of cooking classes in Tokyo, featuring a diverse range of options to cater to every culinary interest.

6. Go Cruising In A Go-Kart

Engaging in a go-kart adventure across downtown Tokyo ranks among the most eccentric and exhilarating experiences one can partake in. Clad in cosplay costumes, you can traverse the vibrant streets of Tokyo for a duration ranging from one to three hours, promising an undeniably amusing endeavor.

Regrettably, my friend Ren and I were unable to partake in this delightful escapade due to our time constraints in obtaining international driver's permits before our trip. If you seek a unique and enjoyable activity in Tokyo, few can rival the sheer enjoyment offered by this quintessentially Japanese experience.

7. Watch Sumo

Observing a sumo tournament or practice session has always been a cherished aspiration of mine during my visits to Japan. My brother and sister-in-law had the opportunity to witness a sumo practice in Tokyo, and they regarded it as one of the most remarkable highlights of their time in Japan.

Ryogoku District, nestled within Sumida Ward, stands as Tokyo's esteemed Sumo Town, housing the renowned Ryogoku Kokugikan sumo stadium, sumo stables, and a multitude of chanko restaurants. Chanko nabe, a hot pot dish consumed by sumo wrestlers to sustain their formidable physiques, is a culinary delicacy associated with this tradition.

Sumo wrestling tournaments are held in January, May, and September. If your visit to Tokyo coincides with these months, consider seizing the opportunity to witness a captivating tournament firsthand.

Alternatively, numerous sumo-related experiences await, such as attending a sumo practice session or relishing a delectable chanko nabe lunch. Platforms like Klook, Get Your Guide, or Magical-Trip provides comprehensive listings of sumo-related activities in Tokyo.

WHERE TO EAT IN TOKYO

As an aficionado of gastronomic exploration, it became imperative for me to curate a comprehensive Tokyo food guide, one that transcended mere recommendations of the city's finest sushi bars or ramen establishments. I aimed to encompass Tokyo's regional culinary landscape, thereby presenting an all-encompassing guide that celebrated the diverse flavors of the city.

The result is this comprehensive Tokyo food guide, featuring 18 must-visit restaurants. If you find yourself pondering where to dine in Tokyo, I hope this curated list of eighteen establishments will guide you toward exceptional culinary experiences.

Considering that eighteen choices might be overwhelming for some, I have highlighted six of our personal favorites below, to offer a well-rounded Tokyo food experience. For more captivating visuals and detailed information about each of these esteemed restaurants, I encourage you to peruse our complete Tokyo food guide.

麺処いのこ平和台店

Unquestionably, one of our most remarkable dining experiences in Tokyo, this neighborhood restaurant astounded us with its unparalleled ramen offerings.

This hidden gem, 麺処いのこ平和台店, was recommended to us by a local Japanese individual who, at first, was hesitant to disclose the information. While he consented to our visit, he requested that we refrain from publicly sharing the details, as the establishment often experiences lengthy queues.

Fortunately, they have three branches, and he graciously allowed us to divulge the address of the branch he does not frequent. Refer to our comprehensive Tokyo travel guide for precise location information.

The crab miso ramen was delectable, but the ebi miso tsukemen left an indelible impression. Infused with the rich umami flavor derived from shrimp heads, it offered an unparalleled gustatory experience. Undoubtedly, it ranks among the finest bowls of ramen we have ever savored.

Sushi Katsura

Finding reasonably priced yet exceptional sushi outside of kaiten-zushi (conveyor belt sushi) restaurants can prove challenging in a city as renowned for its culinary splendor as Tokyo. Fortunately, we discovered Sushi Katsura.

Situated near Tsukiji Outer Market, Sushi Katsura has garnered acclaim as a prime contender for the title of "cheapest good sushi" in Tokyo, as described by one discerning reviewer. For a mere JPY 1,280, I indulged in a lunch sushi set consisting of nine pieces of nigiri, six pieces of maki, and one tamago (sweet rolled omelet).

Sushi Katsura sources its fish from the nearby Tsukiji market, guaranteeing the highest quality and freshness that aficionados of sushi demand.

Houmiya

During my discussion with a Japanese friend regarding notable dining establishments in Tokyo, he emphasized that a conversation about Tokyo food would be incomplete without mentioning monjayaki, which is considered an essential culinary experience unique to Tokyo.

Monjayaki, akin to okonomiyaki, is crafted using pan-fried batter. However, what sets it apart is the addition of dashi or water, resulting in a thinner consistency. Unlike okonomiyaki, when cooked, monjayaki retains a soft and gooey texture, reminiscent of melted cheese.

To savor the finest monjayaki, the Tsukushima area stands out as one of the prime destinations in Tokyo. Hence, following my friend's recommendation, I embarked on a culinary journey to experience monjayaki at Houmiya.

Miyako

Another dish synonymous with Tokyo's culinary heritage is fukagawa meshi. This delectable creation features clams and long onions cooked in miso and served over a bed of rice.

Similar to monjayaki, the quest for the most exceptional rendition of fukagawa meshi necessitates a visit to a specific district within Tokyo. The birthplace of this dish, Fukagawa, continues to uphold its reputation as the ultimate culinary destination for savoring the finest fukagawa meshi.

Historically, Fukagawa was a bustling fishing town, where its inhabitants derived their livelihoods from fishing, clam gathering, and later harvesting. It was during this era that fukagawa meshi emerged as a humble working-class delicacy, cherished even to this day. To indulge in this culinary treasure, one can visit specialty establishments like Miyako in Fukagawa.

Kisaburo Nojo

Kisaburo Nojo is renowned for its expertise in serving tamago kake gohan, a beloved Japanese comfort food consisting of steamed rice topped with raw egg and soy sauce. Comparable to the American classic of peanut butter and jelly, according to my Japanese friend.

At Kisaburo Nojo, guests have the opportunity to partake in an all-you-can-eat tamago kake gohan buffet, featuring premium eggs sourced from various farms across Japan. Not limiting myself to raw eggs and rice, I opted for the tamago kake gohan set with chicken, which offered a clean and flavorful experience, reminiscent of enjoying a raw egg-infused oyakodon.

Savoy

Although it may seem unusual to include a pizzeria in a guide to Japanese cuisine, as mentioned earlier, Tokyo is renowned for its remarkable Neapolitan-style pizzas, rivaling those found in Italy.

Fans of the Ugly Delicious series with David Chang may recognize Savoy as one of the establishments featured in the pizza episode of the show.

Savoy focuses on two types of pizza—the classic Margherita and marinara. While we have yet to visit Italy for a direct comparison, these pizzas easily claimed the title of the best we have ever tasted. Simple yet perfect in every bite.

As aptly expressed by a reviewer, "The best pizza isn't in Italy, it's in Tokyo!" For an authentic Savoy experience, ensure you visit the original branch located in Azabu-juban.

THE 10 BEST HOSTELS IN TOKYO

Tokyo, being one of the world's most expensive cities, requires careful budgeting to make the most of your visit. Fortunately, numerous outstanding and affordable hostels in Tokyo enable you to enjoy your stay while keeping costs in check.

Similar to the city itself, these hostels exude cleanliness, artistic flair, and an abundance of charm. Many of them boast trendy aesthetics and offer standard Wi-Fi connectivity, with some also providing cooking facilities. Bed prices typically range from 2,000 to 5,000 JPY per night, and most hostels organize events, offer an array of tea options, and feature cozy sleeping cubicles.

Whether you seek a tranquil retreat or a vibrant party atmosphere, Tokyo caters to all preferences when it comes to hostels.

Having frequented Tokyo for several years and stayed at numerous accommodations, I understand the factors that influence hostel selection. When evaluating the best hostels in Tokyo, four primary aspects come to the forefront:

Location: Given Tokyo's vast size and the time it may take to navigate the metro system, choosing a centrally located hostel that aligns with your desired attractions and nightlife is crucial. The hostels listed below are all situated in central locations.

Price: In Tokyo, it is important to consider that quality often corresponds with price. Opting for extremely low-priced hostels may result in cramped spaces and subpar service.

Amenities: Every hostel in the city offers complimentary Wi-Fi, and most provide a complimentary breakfast. However, if you desire additional amenities, conducting thorough research will help you find the hostel that best caters to your specific needs.

Staff: The hostels listed below boast exceptional staff members who are friendly and knowledgeable. Even if you ultimately choose an alternative establishment, perusing reviews to ensure you select a hostel with helpful and friendly staff is crucial, as their demeanor can significantly impact your overall experience.

To assist you in planning your trip, I have compiled a list of the best hostels in Tokyo. If you prefer a condensed overview, the following hostels excel in their respective categories:

Best Hostel for Budget Travelers: Nui. Hostel Bar & Lounge

Best Hostel for Families: Unplan Kagurazaka

Best Hostel for Solo Female Travelers: Imano Tokyo Hostel

Best Hostel for Digital Nomads: Hostel Chapter Two Tokyo

Best Hostel for Partying: Hostel Bedgasm

Best Overall Hostel: Hostel Chapter Two Tokyo

For detailed information about each hostel, including prices categorized as follows:

- $ = Under 3,000 JPY
- $$ = 3,000-4,000 JPY
- $$$ = Over 4,000 JPY

1. Sakura Hotel Jimbocho

Situated in a tranquil residential neighborhood, Sakura Hotel Jimbocho enjoys a central location near prominent attractions such as the Imperial Palace and Tokyo Dome. Setting itself apart from other hostels in Tokyo, it offers a complimentary breakfast that includes eggs, toast, and tea/coffee. Additionally, the lobby features a 24/7 bar/cafe where guests can relax and indulge in snacks and refreshments.

The facilities at Sakura Hotel Jimbocho are noteworthy, with excellent shower pressure, comfortable beds, and cozy accommodations featuring privacy curtains for a restful sleep. The range of room options caters to diverse preferences, including single private rooms for solo travelers seeking enhanced privacy, double bedrooms, family rooms accommodating up to five individuals, and classic dormitory rooms.

The dedicated staff at Sakura Hotel Jimbocho extends a warm welcome and goes the extra mile to ensure guest satisfaction. Regularly organized activities throughout the week provide opportunities for socializing with fellow travelers.

Sakura Hotel Jimbocho at a glance:
- Price range: $$

- Complimentary breakfast

- Cafe/bar for socializing and mingling

- Friendly and attentive staff, with organized activities

- Bed prices start from 3,550 JPY and private room prices from 6,300 JPY.

2. Sheena and Ippei

Sheena and Ippei is a boutique hostel conveniently located in downtown Tokyo near Ikebukuro station. The distinctive decor showcases beautiful Japanese fabrics adorning the walls, creating a unique ambiance. The establishment exudes a warm and welcoming atmosphere, and the knowledgeable staff readily provides recommendations for exploring the local area. While there is no kitchen available, guests can utilize the microwave and refrigerator for basic storage and preparation needs.

On the first floor, a charming café equipped with sewing machines accommodates customers, fostering an environment where locals engage in handicrafts and weekly events. In the evenings, the café transforms into a hostel lounge, offering appetizers and sake on weekends—an ideal opportunity to meet fellow travelers.

Sheena and Ippei at a glance:
- Price range: $$$

- Café/lounge for socializing and connecting with others

- Helpful staff offering assistance with trip planning

- Traditional Japanese décor creates a cozy atmosphere

- Bed prices start from 5,000 JPY and private room prices from 11,700 JPY.

3. Hostel Chapter Two Tokyo

Located near Skytree Station in Asakusa, Hostel Chapter Two Tokyo is a small, family-run establishment. The hostel's shared kitchen and common room foster a vibrant social atmosphere, providing ample opportunities for interaction. The dormitories are modern, impeccably maintained, and well-equipped. For added privacy, guests can opt for the deluxe pod, featuring partitioned-off beds with partial walls and privacy curtains—an appealing alternative to the traditional open-concept dormitories with bunk beds.

Guests can enjoy a splendid view of the Sumida River, and it is recommended to secure a bed facing this scenic vista. The rooftop patio offers a co-working space, providing a convenient option for digital nomads seeking relaxation and a conducive work environment. The friendly owner contributes to the hostel's inviting atmosphere.

Hostel Chapter Two Tokyo at a Glance:
• Price range: $$$

• Excellent environment for meeting fellow travelers

• Co-working space catering to digital nomads

• Rooftop patio ideal for relaxation and socializing

• Bed prices start from 5,600 JPY and private room prices from 13,500 JPY.

4. The Millennials Shibuya

The Millennials Shibuya stands out as a modern and well-appointed hostel situated in the heart of Shibuya. While it is the priciest option on this list, it offers a comprehensive range of amenities. The hostel's coworking area features abundant seating, numerous power outlets, and fast Wi-Fi, making it an excellent choice for digital nomads. Private booths are available for conducting calls and meetings.

Every aspect of this hostel, which can be likened to a capsule hotel, exudes a sense of luxury and incorporates high-tech elements. Smart beds that adjust with a simple touch of a button and delightful rain showers contribute to an exceptional guest experience. Complimentary amenities, including slippers, towels, toiletries, charging cables, and adapters, are provided to guests, ensuring a comfortable stay.

Despite the individual private pods, the hostel offers ample spaces for socializing. Additionally, every evening from 5:30 to 6:30 pm, guests can enjoy complimentary beer, providing an ideal opportunity to unwind and connect with fellow travelers after a day of exploration.

The Millennials Shibuya at a glance:
• Price range: $$$

• Complimentary beer served every evening

• Abundance of common areas, including coworking space, social lounge, and rooftop terrace

• Well-equipped kitchen with complimentary coffee/tea and paid breakfast in the morning

• Bed prices starting from 11,400 JPY.

5. Hostel Bedgasm

Situated in East Tokyo, Hostel Bedgasm boasts a vibrant bar where guests are treated to a complimentary drink each evening. This small but thoughtful gesture serves as an excellent opportunity to connect with fellow travelers and foster a social atmosphere. The hostel features clean bathrooms, a communal kitchen, and a tranquil rooftop patio area. Abundant storage space is available for personal belongings, and the staff members are highly attentive and accommodating.

The neighborhood surrounding the hostel offers a pleasant ambiance with a variety of superb dining options, notably the nearby ramen establishment and bakery, which the staff is eager to guide you to. Conveniently, direct metro lines connect Hostel Bedgasm to popular attractions such as Ueno, Ginza, Roppongi, and the Tsukiji fish market.

Although the mattresses may not be exceptionally thick, the beds are equipped with curtains, reading lights, and outlets to ensure comfort and privacy.

Hostel Bedgasm at a Glance:
- Price Range: $$ (Moderate)

- Lively bar with complimentary drinks fostering social interaction

- Serene rooftop patio for relaxation

- Embraces a lively hostel atmosphere

Bed rates start from 3,500 JPY, while private rooms begin at 8,500 JPY.

6. Nui. Hostel & Bar Lounge

Located in the Asakusa area, just a short stroll from Kuritsu Sumida Park along the Sumida River, Nui. Hostel & Bar Lounge shares a commonality with several other establishments on this list. While it may not be situated in the heart of Tokyo, it serves as a respite from the bustling city, requiring approximately 30 minutes of travel time to and from the hostel. The surrounding neighborhood offers a pleasant environment, making it an ideal choice for those seeking tranquility amid Tokyo's vibrant energy. Additionally, Nui. Hostel benefits from direct train access to both airports, ensuring convenient arrivals and departures.

Nui. Hostel is particularly well-suited for travelers who value social interaction without the intensity of a party-oriented atmosphere. The friendly and welcoming staff create a warm atmosphere, and the establishment offers various communal spaces, including a serene lounge on the upper floor and a vibrant cafe/bar on the ground level, which attracts both travelers and locals alike.

Featuring cozy rooms adorned with wooden decor, Nui. Hostel provides a homely ambiance. The beds are comfortable and equipped with personal reading lamps and curtains to ensure privacy. Lockers are available, although guests are advised to bring their locks. In terms of cleanliness, the hostel consistently maintains a high standard, ensuring all facilities, including the bathrooms, are impeccably maintained.

Nui. Hostel & Bar Lounge at a glance:
• Price Range: $ (Affordable)

• Well-regarded local cafe/bar on the premises

• Multiple communal spaces, including a lounge and rooftop terrace

• Fully equipped kitchen for guests' convenience

Bed rates start from 2,600 JPY, while private rooms begin at 6,800 JPY.

7. Imano Tokyo Hostel

Imano Tokyo Hostel presents an excellent choice for those seeking a central location in the heart of all the action. Situated in Shinjuku, one of Tokyo's most vibrant neighborhoods renowned for its bustling nightlife and the iconic Shinjuku Crossing, which holds the distinction of being the world's busiest pedestrian crossing.

While the rooms at Imano Tokyo Hostel may be slightly compact, a common area is available for guests to relax and unwind. Furthermore, a cafe/bar on the premises offers breakfast and coffee in the morning, along with drinks and light snacks in the evening. The beds are new and comfortable, featuring privacy curtains, reading lights, and individual sockets. Female travelers will appreciate the separate floors designated for men, women, and mixed-gender accommodation. Additionally, the rooms are equipped with keypads, eliminating the need to carry physical keys—an added convenience for guests.

Imano Tokyo Hostel at a glance:
- Price Range: $$ (Moderate)

- Convenient central location in Shinjuku

- Cafe/bar and communal area for relaxation

- Modern beds with privacy curtains, reading lights, and outlets

Bed rates start from 3,500 JPY, while private rooms begin at 9,000 JPY.

8. Unplan Kagurazaka

Despite its recent establishment, Unplan Kagurazaka stands out for its cleanliness and stylish ambiance, featuring wooden floors and minimalist decor. The hostel offers a range of room options, catering to solo travelers and families alike, with accommodations ranging from dormitories to four-bed private rooms. On the first floor, a public cafe serves exceptional coffee throughout the day and transforms into a bar in the evening, offering an array of sake and local beers. Additionally, guests can indulge in a complimentary and satisfying breakfast.

Although Unplan Kagurazaka may be relatively more expensive than other hostels, its central location within the city and quality rooms make it a worthwhile choice.

Unplan Kagurazaka at a glance:
- Price Range: $$$ (Higher-end)

- Spacious private rooms ideal for groups and families

- Complimentary hearty breakfast

- On-site cafe/bar for relaxation and socializing

Bed rates start from 4,600 JPY, while private rooms begin at 24,000 JPY.

9. CITAN Hostel

CITAN Hostel is a trendy haven nestled in the Nihonbashi area, epitomizing what one would consider a "boutique" hostel. Boasting seven stories and accommodating 130 beds, the establishment takes pride in maintaining cleanliness, while the invigorating showers provide robust water pressure. The first-floor common area offers a laid-back atmosphere, complemented by a well-equipped kitchen for guests to prepare their meals.

An exceptional addition to the premises is the remarkable coffee shop, Berth Coffee, situated on the first floor, as well as a basement bar and restaurant. Particularly on weekends, the bar thrives with activity, attracting not only hostel guests but also local patrons, often accompanied by a Saturday night DJ. Consequently, the atmosphere is more akin to a lively bar than a traditional hostel, although the peaceful neighborhood guarantees a restful night's sleep. The pod-style beds feature curtains, reading lights, and adequately sized mattresses.

CITAN Hostel at a glance:
• Price range: $$

• Serenely located neighborhood ensuring a peaceful slumber

• On-site bar, restaurant, and café promoting easy socialization

• Exceptional showers with remarkable water pressure

• Bed prices start from 3,600 JPY and private room prices from 9,000 JPY.

10. Toco Tokyo Heritage Hostel
Toco Tokyo Heritage Hostel presents a unique opportunity to experience a night's stay in a traditional 20th-century Japanese

wooden home, complete with a serene central garden and a picturesque koi pond. Meticulously restored both inside and out, the property tastefully blends modern amenities with the elegant simplicity of Japanese design. The wooden bunks, accompanied by plush mattresses and curtains, ensure a comfortable rest.

Situated in a tranquil residential neighborhood, the hostel enjoys a central location with convenient transport links, providing seamless access to Tokyo's various attractions. As a social hub, the hostel features a cozy bar and lounge frequented not only by travelers but also by locals. Furthermore, every hostel guest is treated to a complimentary drink each night. Notably, Toco Tokyo Heritage Hostel offers affordability without compromising on quality, making it an attractive choice for visitors.

Toco Tokyo Heritage Hostel at a Glance:
- Price range: $$$

- Traditional Japanese-style building with a captivating garden

- Bar and lounge offering nightly complimentary drinks

- Dedicated female-only dormitories

PLACES TO VISIT IN TOKYO

The following attractions were among my personal favorites to explore in Tokyo. This list represents only a fraction of the multitude of places you can visit in the city. If you seek further recommendations, please refer to our comprehensive 5-day Tokyo itinerary.

1. Meiji Shrine

Meiji Jingu, also known as Meiji Shrine, holds significant reverence as one of Japan's most esteemed shrines. During the initial days of the new year, over 3 million devotees flock to the shrine to offer their first prayers of the year.

Meiji Shrine stands as a Shinto shrine devoted to the deified spirits of Emperor Meiji and Empress Shoken. Constructed in 1920, eight years after Emperor Meiji's passing, this shrine commemorates the first emperor of modern Japan.

Situated within an expansive 70-hectare forested park adjacent to Yoyogi Park and Harajuku Station, Meiji Shrine is easily accessible for independent visits. Alternatively, guided tours can be arranged through reputable platforms like Klook or Get Your Guide, which offers various tour options featuring Meiji Shrine.

Information at a glance:
Closest Subway Station: Harajuku Station

Admission: Free

Estimated Time to Spend: Approximately 1 – 1.5 hours

2. Senso-ji

Similar to Meiji Shrine, Senso-ji stands as one of Tokyo's most renowned religious landmarks. Established in 645, it proudly holds the distinction of being Tokyo's oldest Buddhist temple, dedicated to the benevolent deity Kannon, the Goddess of Mercy.

Located in Asakusa, a mere minute away from Asakusa Station, Senso-ji is particularly famous for its iconic outer gate, Kaminarimon, which symbolizes both Asakusa and the city of Tokyo. The area between Kaminarimon and Senso-ji is a vibrant stretch adorned with shops offering an assortment of delectable snacks and memorable souvenirs.

Visiting Senso-ji can be done independently or through guided tours. For a comprehensive list of tours and activities in Senso-ji and Asakusa, consider consulting platforms such as Klook and Get Your Guide.

Information at a glance:
Closest Subway Station: Asakusa Station

Admission: Free

Estimated Time to Spend: Approximately 30 minutes – 1 hour

3. Koishikawa Korakuen

Koishikawa Korakuen stands as one of Tokyo's oldest and most captivating landscaped gardens. Dating back to the Edo Period (1600-1867), this garden showcases enchanting walking trails that wind through lush trees, serene ponds, meandering streams, and captivating rock formations.

Koishikawa Korakuen exudes its unique charm throughout the year, with spring and autumn often regarded as the seasons when its beauty reaches its pinnacle. The garden serves as an idyllic retreat, offering a serene respite from the bustling energy of Tokyo.

Information at a glance:

Closest Subway Station: Iidabashi or Suidobashi Station

Admission: JPY 300

Estimated Time to Spend: Approximately 1 – 1.5 hours

4. Tsukiji Outer Market

Tsukiji Outer Market holds the distinction of being Tokyo's most renowned fish market, captivating visitors with its vibrant atmosphere and culinary delights. Located a short 15-minute walk from Ginza Station, this market gained fame for its erstwhile tuna auctions held within the inner market.

While the tuna auctions have been relocated to Toyosu Market, Tsukiji Outer Market remains a bustling hub of activity. It offers a splendid opportunity to immerse oneself in Japan's captivating market culture while savoring an enticing array of seafood and delectable Japanese street food.

Exploring Tsukiji Outer Market can be done independently, or one can opt for market tours available through platforms like Klook, Get Your Guide, byFood, and Magical-Trip, offering a diverse range of Tsukiji Market experiences.

Information at a glance:

Closest Subway Station: Tsukiji or Tsukijishijo Station

Admission: Free

Estimated Time to Spend: Approximately 1 hour

5. teamLab Planets

While no longer open, Borderless was a multimedia exhibit crafted by the teamLab art collective. Occupying a sprawling 100,000 square meter space in Odaiba, it showcased a series of interactive digital displays spread across multiple rooms.

teamLab continues to captivate audiences with another multimedia exhibit near Toyosu Market called Planets. Sharing similarities with Borderless, Planets distinguishes itself through an exhibit that requires visitors to wade through knee-deep water. Tickets for Planets can be obtained through platforms like Klook or GetYourGuide.

Information at a glance:
Closest Subway Station: Shin-Toyosu Station

Admission: JPY 3,200

Estimated Time to Spend: Approximately 2-3 hours

6. MOMAT

MOMAT, an abbreviation for the National Museum of Modern Art, is a dedicated showcase of modern art in Japan, featuring works from the Meiji period onward, as implied by its name.

Spanning four floors, this well-proportioned museum presents a diverse collection of captivating artworks. As someone primarily exposed to traditional Japanese art before visiting, I found it intriguing to witness the influence of Western genres such as cubism and surrealism in the exhibited works.

Information at a glance:
Closest Subway Station: Takebashi Station

Admission: JPY 500

Estimated Time to Spend: Approximately 1.5 – 2 hours

7. Yayoi Kusama Museum

Yayoi Kusama, a renowned Japanese contemporary artist, has gained recognition for her remarkable sculptures and installations adorned with captivating polka dots. While also engaging in other artistic endeavors such as painting and film, her sculptures remain the cornerstone of her artistic oeuvre.

Regrettably, our excitement to visit the museum was met with the realization that purchasing advanced tickets online is an absolute necessity. Due to capacity restrictions, a specific time slot must be selected as only a limited number of visitors are permitted at any given time.

The Yayoi Kusama Museum enjoys immense popularity, resulting in tickets often selling out swiftly. To secure your admission, it is advised to reserve your preferred time slot several weeks in advance through the official Yayoi Kusama Museum website.

Information at a glance:
Closest Subway Station: Ushigome-Yanagicho Station

Admission: JPY 1,100

Estimated Time to Spend: Maximum of 1.5 hours

8. Tokyo Skytree

During our stay in Sumida, we were fortunate to pass by Tokyo Skytree daily. This towering structure serves as a television broadcasting tower and currently stands as the tallest edifice in Japan.

Impressively reaching a height of 634 meters, Tokyo Skytree boasts two observation decks situated at 350 and 450 meters respectively, offering breathtaking panoramic views of the cityscape. Tickets for the observation decks can be purchased directly at the entrance or conveniently obtained in advance through the Klook platform.

Information at a glance:

Closest Subway Station: Oshiage Station

Admission: Ticketing information is available

Estimated Time to Spend: Approximately 1 hour

CHAPTER FIVE

TRANSPORTATION HOW TO GET TO AND AROUND JAPAN?

GETTING TO JAPAN

Major international flights originating from regions such as Europe, North America, Australia, and New Zealand predominantly arrive at either Tokyo's Narita International Airport or Osaka's Kansai International Airport. These strategically located airports near their respective cities serve as vital global gateways for Japan's prominent airlines.

To secure the most competitive fares, we recommend purchasing tickets at least six weeks in advance. Should you require assistance in determining the most suitable travel route, please feel free to contact our team for personalized recommendations.

GETTING AROUND JAPAN

The renowned Shinkansen, also known as the Japanese bullet train, presents a seamless and expeditious mode of transportation for traversing the entire country, sparing you the inconvenience of potential flight delays and airport commutes. Shinkansen bullet trains conveniently interconnect numerous cities, including the popular Tokyo to Kyoto route, which can be covered in a mere two and a half hours. Each Shinkansen line boasts a variety of train options, affording customers the freedom to select their preferred experience.

It is worth noting that train travel in Japan may pose limitations on accommodating larger luggage beyond carry-on suitcase size. However, many hotels offer a valuable service whereby they can arrange for the delivery of your luggage to your subsequent destination, alleviating any concerns regarding storage constraints.

HOW TO GET AROUND IN JAPAN (EVEN IF YOU DON'T SPEAK JAPANESE): UNDERSTANDING BULLET TRAINS, BUSES, BIKES AND MORE

Navigating Japan's vast and diverse landscape can initially seem daunting due to its numerous islands, bustling cities, mountain ranges, and national parks. However, with a closer look, you'll discover that traveling within Japan is a delightful experience, whether utilizing trains, ferries, or renting vehicles. Here is our comprehensive guide to getting around Japan.

THE TRAIN IS BEST FOR INTERCITY TRAVEL

Trains are the most popular and highly recommended means of transportation for travelers exploring Japan. They offer speed, efficiency, and exceptional reliability, ensuring a stress-free journey to virtually any destination within the country.

Japan Railways (JR) is the primary operator, encompassing a network of interconnected rail systems throughout Japan. The renowned shinkansen, or bullet train, routes operated by JR connect major cities at speeds reaching nearly 320km/h (200mph). Additionally, a vast network of private railways serves each large city, along with its surrounding areas. Some sleeper train services are still operational, providing unique travel experiences.

Major train stations are well-signposted in English, and announcements on long-haul trains are made in both Japanese and English. The main challenge for travelers is navigating the sometimes labyrinthine stations, which may have multiple routes. Allocating sufficient time for transfers is advisable.

HOW TO BUY TRAIN TICKETS IN JAPAN
Train tickets can be purchased through touch-screen vending machines found in major train stations (many have an English function), at the midori-no-madoguchi counter, at JR's in-house travel agency located in major JR stations, or at travel agencies within train stations. Japan Travel Bureau (JTB) branches are widely available throughout the country. Ticket prices are comparable to train fares in Western Europe, with faster services commanding higher prices than slower trains.

Seat reservations are mandatory for Shinkansen and certain tokkyū (limited express) lines. These reservations can be made from one month in advance up until the day of departure. Unreserved tickets, which do not guarantee a specific seat, are also available and generally do not sell out, although seating may become limited during peak periods.

Many visitors opt for rail passes, such as the popular Japan Rail Pass, which offers unlimited rides on all JR services for durations of seven, 14, or 21 days. The seven-day pass costs approximately ¥33,700 (around US$300). Regional passes, such as the Tōhoku Area Pass or Tokyo Wide Pass, are available for travelers focusing on specific areas of the country. Details about various passes can be obtained from the respective JR Railways websites (JR Central, JR East, JR West), although passes outside the JR network are also available.

BUS TRAVEL IS THE BEST BUDGET OPTION

Japan boasts an extensive network of long-distance buses connecting the islands of Honshū, Shikoku, and Kyūshū. Although not as fast as the Shinkansen, buses offer a more affordable option for budget-conscious travelers and cover routes that trains do not.

Japan Railways (JR) operates the largest highway bus network in the country, often departing from and arriving at train stations rather than bus stops in cities. While slightly pricier, JR buses are known for their reliability. Other reputable operators, such as Willer Express, offer more affordable options. Japan Bus Lines, a service provided by the company, allows travelers to book seats on Willer and other operators.

Night bus services are available for most long-haul routes. Premium coaches feature spacious seats that recline significantly, providing a comfortable overnight journey and a cost-effective alternative to accommodation. These buses typically arrive at their destinations in the early morning, around 6 am or 7 am. All buses are equipped with onboard toilets for convenience.

HIRING A CAR OR MOTORCYCLE GIVES THE MOST FLEXIBILITY

When traveling to rural areas in Japan, hiring a car is the most convenient mode of transportation, particularly for groups of two or more individuals. Exploring regions such as Hokkaidō, Tōhoku, Hida, Shirakawa-gō, the Japan Alps, the Noto Peninsula (Central Honshū), the San-in Coast (Western Honshū), Shikoku, Kyūshū, and Okinawa is best experienced by car.

Driving in Japan has been made easier with the availability of navigation systems. However, it is important to note that in remote mountainous areas, the reliability of these systems may be limited. Therefore, it is advisable to allocate ample time to locate your intended destination.

When renting vehicles, prices among agencies are generally comparable, starting from approximately ¥7000 per day (US$60) for a compact car, with discounts offered for rentals extending beyond a single day. Prominent rental companies such as Nippon and Toyota have extensive networks throughout Japan and provide vehicles equipped with English-language navigation systems. Online bookings can be conveniently completed in English.

Renting a motorcycle for long-distance touring presents certain challenges compared to hiring a car. However, Rental 819 is among the few agencies that facilitate English bookings. Scooter rentals are more commonly available on smaller islands, requiring an international license (not necessarily a motorcycle license) for rental. It is important to note that wearing helmets is mandatory for motorcyclists in Japan.

WHAT TO EXPECT ON THE ROAD

Japanese roads are generally well-maintained and in excellent condition. Roadworks in progress are more commonly encountered than roads requiring repair. Keep in mind that mountain roads and many urban roads tend to be narrow, and navigating one-way streets is also a consideration in cities.

Winter driving in Japan can be hazardous for those without experience in snowy and icy conditions. Snowfall can occur in higher elevations as early as November (October in Hokkaidō) and may lead to temporary closures of mountain passes, which could persist until April. While roads in Japan are typically signposted in English, weather warnings and road closures may not always be readily available. If planning to drive through mountainous areas during winter, it is advisable to have someone (possibly at your accommodation) verify the feasibility of your route given the current conditions.

YOU MAY NEED TO TRANSLATE YOUR DRIVING LICENSE

Travelers from most countries can drive (both cars and motorcycles) in Japan by presenting an International Driving Permit alongside their regular driver's license. However, residents of select countries may need to obtain an authorized translation of their license. Branches of the Japan Automobile Federation (JAF) offer same-day translations for ¥3000 (US$26).

MOST CITIES HAVE DOMESTIC AIRPORTS, SO FLYING IS QUICK AND CHEAP

Air services in Japan are extensive, reliable, and safe, providing a viable alternative to shinkansen (bullet trains). Flying is often faster and occasionally more cost-effective, although it offers fewer opportunities to experience the captivating Japanese scenery up close while also contributing more to environmental impact. Japan Airlines, including Hokkaidō Air System (HAC) and Okinawa carrier Japan Trans Ocean Air (JTA), operates the most extensive domestic network, with All Nippon Airways as the second largest carrier. The majority of cities in Japan have domestic airports.

Both All Nippon Airways (ANA) and Japan Airlines (JAL) offer discounts of up to 50% for tickets purchased one month or more in advance, with smaller discounts available for bookings made one to three weeks in advance.

SOME CITIES OPERATE BIKE-SHARE SCHEMES

Several cities, including Tokyo, Osaka, Kōbe, and Sapporo, offer bike-share schemes. These programs may require advanced online registration and following specific instructions outlined on the respective websites. Bicycles are commonly used by locals for urban transportation, and while Japanese law stipulates that bicycles should be ridden on roads, many people utilize sidewalks. Dedicated cycle lanes are limited in availability. Both drivers and pedestrians generally demonstrate considerate behavior. In urban areas, bicycles should be parked at designated ports or bicycle parking areas.

Bicycles are often available for rent in tourist areas. These rentals typically consist of sturdy, single-speed shopping bikes, although some locations may offer electric bicycles. Child-sized bicycles are not commonly found. As part of local tourism initiatives, bicycles may be available free of charge, while private businesses, usually located near train stations, offer rental services for approximately ¥1000 (US$9) per day. Inquire at local tourist information centers for further details. Many youth hostels also provide bicycle rental or borrowing services.

Children 12 years and under are required to wear helmets while cycling. Adults typically do not wear helmets unless engaged in road touring, and rental shops generally do not provide them (unless children's bicycles are offered, in which case helmets for children will be included in the rental). Please note that it is challenging to rent touring bicycles in Japan, although Cycle Osaka is one operator that offers such services. To transport bicycles on trains, they must be disassembled and stored in bike bags.

BOAT AND FERRY RIDES CAN BE SLOW BUT MEMORABLE
Ferries are typically not the most economical means of transportation and often consume more time. However, the actual boat rides themselves can be quite memorable. Long-haul ferries in Japan feature communal bathhouses, dining halls, and even karaoke rooms.

On overnight ferry journeys, second-class accommodations involve sleeping in communal rooms on plastic mats or the floor. However, it is possible to pay a small additional fee to upgrade to a dormitory or even a suite, which comes at a higher cost. Most major ferry companies have English websites for ticket bookings. Alternatively, travel agencies such as JTB can assist with ferry reservations.

THERE'S A MIXED APPROACH TO ACCESSIBLE TRANSPORTATION IN JAPAN

Japan's approach to accessibility, known as "bariafurī" in Japanese, receives mixed evaluations. Despite potential language barriers, service staff are generally accommodating and willing to assist. Train stations in cities often provide lifts, and station staff are available to aid passengers with temporary slopes when boarding and disembarking trains. However, navigating rural stations can be more challenging.

In terms of infrastructure, newer buildings commonly feature access ramps and wheelchair-accessible toilets. Even major attractions tend to offer accessibility options, although they may not be immediately apparent. For instance, shrines and temples often have rear entrances equipped with ramps. However, it is worth noting that what is considered "accessible" at some sights may still involve steep slopes or lengthy gravel paths.

Certain mid-range to high-end hotels offer one or two barrier-free rooms, but it is advisable to book well in advance. It is essential to review the specific details of what constitutes barrier-free accommodations as definitions may vary. If the need for a wheelchair arises upon arrival, hotel staff can assist with rental arrangements.

Despite these efforts, there are some limitations. Many neighborhoods in Japanese cities lack sidewalks, and restaurants frequently lack sufficient space to accommodate wheelchair users. Seeking out "shōtengai" (market streets), which are often pedestrian-only covered arcades, can be a viable option in most cities.

For comprehensive information on accessibility in Japan, Accessible Japan is a valuable resource that offers an e-book with detailed insights. Additionally, Lonely Planet provides a free Accessible Travel guide to further assist travellers.

Georgia Tucker

CHAPTER SIX

MUST-TRY LOCAL JAPANESE FOODS

In recent decades, Japan has left an indelible mark on the cultural landscape of the UK and other Western countries. Beyond its advancements in automotive, technological, and animated industries, Japan has also enriched our culinary awareness with its delectable and distinct cuisine. As fervent advocates of Japanese gastronomy, we, at Japan Centre, have compiled a definitive list of 30 must-try Japanese foods that transcend boundaries and deserve everyone's attention.

1. Sushi

Undoubtedly, sushi stands as one of the iconic ambassadors of Japanese cuisine. Following the Meiji Restoration in 1868, it became one of the first Japanese dishes to captivate American palates and has since experienced a continuous surge in popularity. The term "sushi" encompasses various dishes featuring Japanese rice seasoned with vinegar. Common iterations include makizushi (rolled sushi with rice and fillings wrapped in nori seaweed), nigiri sushi (hand-pressed mounds of sushi rice topped with single slices of raw fish), and inarizushi (sushi rice enveloped within seasoned, fried tofu pouches).

2. Udon

Among the triumvirate of predominant Japanese noodles, udon noodles reign supreme. These thick and chewy strands, traditionally crafted from wheat flour and brine water, offer versatility in culinary applications. Udon can be incorporated into stir-fries, or hot pots, or served cold with a side of tsuyu or tentsuyu soup for dipping. Most notably, they feature in nourishing noodle soups, accompanied by savory broth and a variety of garnishes. Popular renditions include kitsune udon (topped with aburaage fried tofu), tempura udon (enhanced with tempura-battered seafood and vegetables), and chikara udon (accented with grilled mochi rice cakes).

3. Tofu

While tofu is often associated with health-conscious or vegetarian fare in Western countries, it occupies a prominent place in the everyday diet of Southeast Asian nations like Japan. Tofu, particularly the silky variety, holds broad appeal and is enjoyed by individuals from all walks of life. Produced by coagulating soy milk and pressing the resulting curds into blocks, tofu manifests in varying degrees of firmness. It can be savored uncooked with complementary seasonings, simmered in hot pots, or fried to create flavorful aburaage garnishes.

4. Tempura

If you appreciate the crispiness of deep-fried delicacies, tempura will surely captivate your taste buds. Tempura consists of morsels or slices of meat, fish, and/or vegetables coated in a specialized batter and fried to a delectably crunchy and pale golden hue.

In contrast to the British preference for meat and fish in batter, Japanese tempura primarily features small shellfish like prawns or a diverse array of vegetables, including green beans, pumpkin, daikon mooli radish, and sweet potato. Tempura can be savored on its own, accompanied by grated daikon and a dipping sauce known as tsuyu, or served atop rice bowls or noodle soups, adding texture and flavor to the dish.

5. Yakitori

In the United Kingdom, it is common to opt for chips or a hot dog during a sports match, whereas the Japanese prefer to indulge in yakitori. Yakitori, meaning "barbecued chicken" in literal translation, comprises small skewers of bite-sized chicken pieces that are either seasoned with salt or coated with a sauce, known as tare, made from mirin rice wine, soy sauce, sake, and sugar.

Yakitori encompasses various types, with momo (chicken thigh), Negima (chicken and spring onion), and tsukune (chicken meatballs) being the most prevalent variations.

6. Sashimi

Sashimi, a dish that often sparks debate, consists of expertly sliced raw fish or meat, usually accompanied by daikon radish, pickled ginger, wasabi, and soy sauce. Unlike sushi, which incorporates vinegared rice and may not always feature raw fish, sashimi exclusively consists of raw fish and is never served with rice. To ensure both taste and safety, the fish used in sashimi must be exceptionally fresh, minimizing the risk of contamination and enhancing its flavor.

7. Ramen

Ramen, a beloved noodle soup in present-day Japan, consists of wheat noodles (commonly known as "ramen noodles"), a flavorful broth (typically soy sauce, salt, miso, or tonkotsu pork bone), and various toppings such as sliced pork, nori seaweed, spring onions, bamboo shoots, and more. This delectable dish holds a prominent place in Japanese cuisine, renowned for its affordability and widespread availability in restaurants and ramen bars, which can be found on almost every street corner. The popularity of Japanese ramen is such that Tokyo even houses a ramen-themed museum/amusement park.

8. Donburi

Donburi, a rice bowl dish, rivals ramen in popularity in Japan and is a common choice for busy Japanese workers during lunchtime. Donburi involves preparing various meats, fish, and vegetables by simmering or frying and serving them over steamed rice in large bowls, also referred to as "donburi." While the assortment of ingredients can vary, the most popular types include oyakodon (simmered chicken, egg, and green onion), gyudon (sliced beef and onion simmered in a soy sauce soup base), tendon (tempura pieces fried and drizzled with tsuyu), and katsudon (breaded and deep-fried pork cutlets, or tonkatsu, simmered in tsuyu with onion and egg).

9. Natto

Similar to how Marmite polarizes opinions among the British, natto elicits divided responses from the Japanese. This traditional Japanese food is produced by fermenting soybeans with a specific type of bacteria naturally found in the human gastrointestinal tract. Natto possesses a distinct aroma reminiscent of aged cheese and a sticky, slimy texture that some find unappealing. However, others appreciate these fermented soybeans for their robust, salty, and savory (umami) flavor profile, as well as their abundant nutritional value. Whether natto is deemed delicious or repugnant remains a subjective judgment.

10. Oden

No cold Japanese winter is complete without oden. This winter hot pot dish, known as nabemono, involves simmering an assortment of vegetables and proteins (such as processed fish cakes, mochi rice cakes, boiled eggs, daikon radish, konjac yam, and tofu) in a light broth seasoned with soy sauce and dashi (a soup stock made from infusions of bonito fish flakes, kombu kelp seaweed, and other savory ingredients) in a large hot pot placed at the center of the table. Diners can then select their preferred pieces from the pot and enjoy them with karashi mustard and other condiments. Besides serving as a satisfying main meal, the simmering hot pot also acts as a communal source of warmth on chilly evenings.

11. Tamagoyaki

Tamagoyaki, a culinary gem suitable for any mealtime, epitomizes the art of the Japanese omelet. This delicacy entails meticulously layering and rolling multiple sheets of beaten egg, occasionally seasoned with soy sauce and/or sugar. Upon completion, a freshly cooked tamagoyaki presents itself as a neatly rolled crêpe-like creation. It can be relished as a standalone dish, often enjoyed at breakfast, or employed as a delectable topping or filling in sushi. Notably, tamagoyaki-adorned nigiri sushi serves as a final course in sushi bars, boasting a subtle sweetness that borders on dessert-like indulgence.

12. Soba

Soba, commonly known as "buckwheat noodles" (with "soba" denoting "buckwheat" in Japanese), stands as one of the primary noodle varieties frequently savored in Japan. Distinguished from udon and ramen, soba noodles are crafted using partially, if not entirely, buckwheat flour, imparting them a distinct earthiness and a subtle nutty essence that harmonizes splendidly with robust flavors like garlic and sesame.

Soba can be relished steaming hot in soups adorned with an array of toppings such as spring onions, agetama tempura flakes, kamaboko fish cakes, or grilled mochi. Alternatively, it can be enjoyed cold, accompanied by a side of tsuyu dipping sauce, and garnished with green onions, shredded nori seaweed, and a hint of wasabi.

13. Tonkatsu

Tonkatsu, succulent pork cutlets, stands among the pantheon of yoshoku, or "western-style," dishes that were originally introduced to Japan by Europeans. True to their innovative spirit, the Japanese embraced tonkatsu, transforming it into a culinary masterpiece of their own. This exquisite preparation involves encasing pork chops in crispy panko breadcrumbs, expertly deep-frying them to a golden brown hue. Served with a drizzle of fruit-and-vegetable-based tonkatsu sauce and accompanied by shredded cabbage and other refreshing salad greens, tonkatsu captivates the palate. It is often relished as part of a bento boxed lunch, incorporated into a Japanese curry known as "katsu curry," or cherished as a filling for sandwiches.

14. Kashi Pan

The Japanese possess an affinity for delectable bread rolls, evident in the abundance of bakeries gracing the streets of Japan's bustling cities, rivaling the presence of ramen bars. "Kashipan," meaning "sweet bread," encompasses a variety of single-serve bread buns that originated in Japan. Among the most beloved selections are a melon pan, featuring a bread bun topped with a cookie dough crust, and a pan, a bread bun filled with anko, a delightful sweet red bean paste. Another enticing option is the aree pan or kare pan, which showcases a bread bun brimming with curry sauce, enveloped in panko breadcrumbs, and deep-fried to perfection. Bread enthusiasts, in particular, should not miss the opportunity to indulge in the irresistible charm of Kashipan.

15. Sukiyaki

Similar to oden, sukiyaki reigns as a beloved Japanese nabemono hot pot dish, frequently savored during the winter season. This delectable creation entails searing beef slices in a hot pot, subsequently complemented by sukiyaki broth, typically crafted from a harmonious blend of soy sauce, sake, mirin rice wine, and sugar. Various vegetables, noodles, and proteins find their way into this delightful concoction. True to its name, which translates to "cook what you like," sukiyaki offers a unique dining experience as diners actively participate in its preparation, selecting preferred ingredients and personalizing the flavors at the table.

16. Miso Soup

Few dishes hold as steadfast a position in Japanese cuisine as miso soup. A harmonious combination of miso paste, a traditional fermented soybean delicacy, and dashi broth, miso soup graces the table as a ubiquitous accompaniment to traditional Japanese-style breakfasts, lunches, and dinners. The intricate umami flavors of this soup serve to elevate the culinary experience, enhancing the richness of the main dishes it accompanies. To enhance the body of miso soup, it is customary to incorporate complementary toppings such as green onion, wakame seaweed, and firm tofu, elevating the sensory pleasure derived from this timeless culinary masterpiece.

17. Okonomiyaki

Okonomiyaki is prepared by combining batter, sliced cabbage, and other savory ingredients, and then cooking the mixture on a hot plate, similar to the process of making pancakes. Originating from Osaka and Hiroshima (where a distinct "layered" style of okonomiyaki exists), its popularity has extended throughout Japan, leading to the establishment of specialized okonomiyaki restaurants that are easily accessible.

Certain restaurants even provide the opportunity for patrons to cook their okonomiyaki, offering a delightful and interactive culinary experience.

18. Mentaiko

For enthusiasts of briny seafood, mentaiko is a culinary delight. This savory delicacy involves marinating the roe (fish eggs) of pollock and cod in various salty, flavorful, and sometimes spicy seasonings. While basic mentaiko is marinated in a simple salt solution, the popularity of "karoshi mentaiko" has been growing, characterized by its spicy chili pepper infusion.

Traditionally, mentaiko is enjoyed as a side dish alongside steamed rice, as a topping for ramen, or as a filling within onigiri rice balls. In recent years, mentaiko has also been creatively combined with butter or cream to create a simple yet savory or spicy mentaiko pasta sauce.

19. Nikujaga

Nikujaga is a delectable savory dish consisting of meat, potatoes, and assorted vegetables simmered in a blend of soy sauce, sake, mirin, and sugar. Belonging to the "nimono" category of Japanese cuisine, which translates to "simmered things," nikujaga is commonly found in Japanese restaurants. However, it is also regarded as a homely dish with flavors that can vary from one household to another. For an authentic experience of Japanese nikujaga, the ideal approach is to be invited to a Japanese friend's home and make a special request to their skilled family chef.

20. Curry Rice

Known as "kare" or "kare raisu" in Japanese, Japanese curry is a yoshoku dish that was initially introduced to Japan by the British during the Meiji era (1868-1912). Japanese curry differs from the Indian varieties familiar in the UK, as it generally exhibits a sweeter flavor profile, and a thicker texture, and is prepared more akin to a stew, with meat and vegetables cooked together by boiling in water.

Japanese households often rely on curry roux, solid blocks of Japanese curry paste, to simplify the preparation process. This roux melts into the stew, thickening it to create a flavorsome curry sauce.

21. Unagi no Kabayaki

"Unagi" refers to freshwater eel in Japanese, and unagi no kabayaki represents a popular dish featuring grilled eel that traces its origins back to the Edo period (1603-1868) when kabayaki-style unagi was traditionally consumed during the summer to provide stamina.

To prepare unagi no kabayaki, prepped eel fillets are brushed with a sweetened soy sauce-based kabayaki sauce and then broiled on a grill. The term "kabayaki" denotes this specific grilling method, which can also be applied to other fish types, including catfish. However, while in Japan during the summer, it is recommended to savor the authentic unagi no kabayaki experience.

22. Shabu shabu hot pot

Shabu shabu is a type of nabemono hot pot dish that bears a resemblance to sukiyaki. It involves the gentle boiling of vegetables, tofu, and other ingredients in a flavorful broth infused with kombu kelp seasoning. Thin slices of meat are then delicately dipped into the brothand, swirled around until they are cooked to perfection (typically within a span of 10-20 seconds).

Following this cooking process, the meat is further enhanced by dipping it in a savory ponzu citrus seasoned soy sauce or sesame sauce, before being savored alongside the other boiled ingredients.

The term "shabu shabu" itself derives from an onomatopoeic expression that mimics the sound produced when the meat slices are skillfully swished in the broth.

23. Onigiri

Similar to how the sandwich is considered the quintessential portable food in British cuisine, the onigiri rice ball holds that distinction in Japan. Referred to as 'omusubi,' 'nigirimeshi,' or simply 'rice balls,' onigiri consists of portions of Japanese rice shaped into triangular or cylindrical forms, with a filling nestled within, and enveloped in nori seaweed. This delectable delicacy has been savored in Japan for centuries, and modern Japanese convenience stores offer a diverse selection of onigiri, typically priced between 100-150 yen (£0.75-£1.12) per piece. Popular onigiri fillings include umeboshi pickled plums, seasoned seaweed, tuna mayonnaise, and teriyaki chicken.

24. Gyoza

Gyoza, the crescent-shaped culinary treasures, are savory dumplings filled with a minced combination of ingredients such as pork, cabbage, green onion, and mushrooms (though alternative fillings can also be utilized). Encased in circular gyoza wrappers, these delectable parcels are meticulously crimped or pleated along the edges, resulting in their iconic half-moon shape. Gyoza dumplings are typically prepared by first frying one side to achieve a crisp and flavorful base, followed by steaming for 2-3 minutes to ensure a smooth and silky texture throughout the remaining wrapper, while the filling inside remains moist and succulent.

25. Takoyaki

Within the realm of Japanese street vendor fare, few options rival the notoriety of takoyaki. Referred to as 'octopus balls' or 'octopus dumplings,' this delicacy is skillfully crafted using a unique hot plate featuring rows of half-spherical molds. Each mold is filled with a savory batter mixture before a delectable morsel of tako octopus meat is placed at the center. The takoyaki spheres are then diligently turned with a pick or skewer at regular intervals, ensuring even cooking and yielding perfectly spherical dumplings. Once cooked, they are typically served in batches of six, eight, or ten, brushed with a delectable sweet and savory takoyaki sauce, and adorned with mayonnaise, aonori seaweed, and katsuobushi bonito fish flakes.

26. Kaiseki Ryori

For those seeking the Japanese equivalent of haute cuisine, kaiseki ryori is an experience to savor. Also known simply as 'kaiseki,' this traditional multi-course Japanese dinner embodies the epitome of gastronomic excellence. A complete kaiseki feast comprises a dozen or more meticulously crafted dishes, showcasing fresh, seasonal, and locally sourced produce. Each course is served in small portions, meticulously prepared to enhance the inherent flavors of the ingredients. Kaiseki is a culinary art form, as every course demonstrates a different cooking technique. These exquisite dining experiences are typically enjoyed in specialized restaurants or at ryoka`n, Japanese-style inns.

27. Edamame

Just as frequent patrons of UK pubs often indulge in peanuts and pork scratchings alongside their lagers, regulars at Japan's izakaya pubs delight in freshly prepared edamame. These vibrant green, immature soybeans, harvested before the beans have hardened, are typically served in their pods after being blanched and lightly salted. Beyond their naturally delicious and mellow umami flavor, edamame beans offer various health benefits, being naturally rich in protein, iron, and calcium. It is common for edamame to be served as a complimentary appetizer in pubs and restaurants, adding a delightful touch to the dining experience.

28. Yakisoba

It is virtually impossible to attend a summer festival in Japan and not come across a yakisoba stand.

Attending a summer festival in Japan without encountering a yakisoba stand is nearly impossible. Yakisoba, a delectable fried noodle dish, is prepared by barbecuing or stir-frying a delightful medley of noodles, sliced cabbage, pork, carrots, assorted vegetables, and a savory yakisoba sauce with barbecue undertones. At summer festivals, these ingredients are generously piled onto outdoor hotplates and grilled to perfection. However, yakisoba can also be easily crafted at home using a large frying pan or wok. It is worth noting that while the term "yakisoba" translates to "cooked soba," the noodles used in yakisoba differ from traditional soba noodles, as they do not contain buckwheat.

29. Chawanmushi

As far as mellow, comforting, and uniquely Japanese dishes are concerned, chawanmushi is one of the best.

Among the array of mellow, comforting, and distinctly Japanese dishes, chawanmushi stands out as a true delight. This steamed savory egg custard is created by pouring seasoned, beaten eggs into individual cups that already contain a delightful assortment of meats and vegetables, including chicken, mushrooms, gingko nuts, kamaboko fish cakes, and carrots. The cups are then carefully steamed in a pot or steamer until the custard sets, resulting in a pudding-like texture. The name "chawanmushi" is derived from combining the words "chawan" (referring to a teacup) and "mushi" (meaning "steamed"), thus literally translating to "steamed in a cup."

30. Wagashi

The most authentic way to finish off a Japanese meal or matcha tea ceremony is with wagashi.

A splendid conclusion to a Japanese meal or a matcha tea ceremony is none other than wagashi. Wagashi encompasses a variety of traditional Japanese sweets that originated during the Edo period and are heavily influenced by local ingredients and flavors. These exquisite treats are crafted using a select range of ingredients, including mochi rice cakes, anko paste (sweet red bean paste), kanten (agar, a vegetarian thickener similar to gelatin), chestnuts, and sugar. Notable examples of wagashi include dango (sweet mochi balls skewered on sticks, often served with sugar syrup), daifuku (mochi rice filled with anko), dorayaki (anko sandwiched between two thick pancakes), and yokan (blocks of anko solidified with kanten and sugar).

15 TYPES OF RESTAURANTS IN JAPAN THAT ARE GREAT FOR TOURISTS

Ramen

Ramen comprises a hearty bowl of noodles immersed in a savory broth made from meat. Common toppings include pork slices, bean sprouts, seaweed, and bamboo shoots. Each ramen establishment offers its unique variation of the soup, contributing to the distinct popularity of certain restaurants. Ramen varieties often include soy sauce, salt, or miso as key flavor profiles.

Udon and Soba

Udon and soba dishes are served in both hot and cold preparations. Cold versions typically involve dipping the noodles in a flavorful sauce, while hot variations pair well with toppings such as tempura or kitsune (sweet tofu). Udon noodles are crafted from wheat flour, resulting in thicker, whiter strands with a chewy texture. In contrast, soba noodles consist of buckwheat flour, although they are often a blend of buckwheat and wheat flour.

Sushi

Various types of sushi establishments cater to diverse preferences, with kaiten-zushi emerging as a favored option among tourists. At kaiten-zushi restaurants, sushi plates gracefully circulate on a conveyor belt, allowing patrons to select enticing offerings. However, it is important to exercise discretion when choosing, as the final bill is determined by the number of plates accumulated at your table. It is advisable to take only what you intend to consume.

Yakitori

Yakitori, meaning "grilled chicken," entails expertly grilling skewers laden with delectable combinations of meat and vegetables over a bed of charcoal embers. While chicken variations like teriyaki, salted, or with onions are commonly enjoyed, other ingredients such as pork, bell peppers, mushrooms, asparagus, and garlic also find their way onto these savory skewers.

Yakiniku

Yakiniku, denoting "grilled meat," presents a Korean-inspired barbecue experience featuring a tabletop grill. The server provides raw meat and vegetables, allowing guests to cook the food to their desired level of doneness. Accompanying the spread are an array of tantalizing dipping sauces, enhancing the flavors and offering a customizable dining experience.

Tonkatsu

Tonkatsu establishments specialize in deep-fried, breaded pork cutlets, accompanied by unlimited servings of rice, miso soup, and cabbage. Notable pork cuts include "hire," which refers to a lean and tenderloin portion, and "rosu," denoting a pork loin with a higher fat content, offering different flavor profiles to suit individual preferences.

Okonomiyaki

Okonomiyaki often likened to a Japanese pancake or pizza, defies conventional notions of these culinary classics. Customizable ingredients of choice, ranging from cheese, kimchi, pork, and octopus to shrimp, are incorporated into a batter comprising flour, egg, and water, along with the addition of cabbage. The resulting mixture is poured onto a heated griddle, and the cooked creation is garnished with parsley, soy sauce, mayonnaise, and bonito flakes, providing a harmonious blend of flavors and textures.

Tempura

Tempura involves the art of deep-frying seafood and vegetables in a delicate and airy batter comprising flour, egg, and water. Frequently encountered varieties include shrimp, squid, fish, eggplant, mushrooms, pumpkin, and sweet potato. This cooking method yields a crispy and light texture, accentuating the inherent qualities of the ingredients.

Izakaya

Izakaya establishments epitomize the vibrant fusion of a Japanese bar and grill, offering an extensive array of culinary delights amidst a lively and animated ambiance. Edamame, pickled vegetables, sashimi (raw fish), yakitori, salads, fried chicken, french fries, and even pizza grace the menu, encouraging a shared dining experience with dishes ordered for the entire table.

Curry

Japanese curry, akin to the beloved macaroni and cheese in American cuisine, holds a cherished place as a delightful and easily relished dish, even among younger palates. Distinguished by its thicker consistency, gentle sweetness, and milder spice levels compared to Indian or Thai curries, Japanese curry typically incorporates pork or beef as a base, accompanied by carrots, potatoes, and onions, resulting in a comforting and flavorsome ensemble.

Unagi

Specializing in freshwater eel, unagi restaurants masterfully grill the eel over charcoal, imparting a smoky essence. The succulent eel is then crowned with a luscious and rich soy-based sauce before being served atop a bed of rice, creating a harmonious marriage of flavors and textures.

Sukiyaki and Shabu Shabu

During the winter season, sukiyaki and shabu shabu establishments attract enthusiasts seeking a heartwarming dining experience. Both styles involve communal pot cooking at the table, featuring thinly sliced meat, leafy vegetables, shiitake mushrooms, and tofu. Sukiyaki presents a sweet soy sauce-based broth, while shabu shabu offers a clear and kelp-infused broth, allowing guests to savor the essence of the ingredients in their preferred culinary fashion.

Yatai

Yatai is street-side food stalls that offer a unique dining experience. These stalls often provide seating arrangements with stools, tables, and occasionally tents. They specialize in a variety of dishes, including okonomiyaki, ramen, takoyaki, yakisoba, and yakitori.

Shokudo

Shokudo refers to small, typically family-run restaurants or cafeterias located near train stations and tourist attractions. These establishments serve an array of affordable Japanese dishes, such as curry, ramen, soba, udon, and tempura. Additionally, they typically offer a daily special that includes rice and miso soup.

Fast Food

Japan is home to numerous fast-food restaurants, encompassing both American chains like McDonald's, Burger King, Kentucky Fried Chicken, and Subway, as well as indigenous Japanese fast food chains. Mos Burger, one of the most popular hamburger restaurants in Japan, offers an extensive menu featuring beef burgers, rice burgers, soy burgers, lettuce wraps, hot dogs, french fries, and onion rings.

CHAPTER SEVEN

DISCOVERING HOKKAIDO

WELCOME TO HOKKAIDO

THE BEST THINGS TO DO IN HOKKAIDO

1. See the Amazing Ice Sculptures At The Sapporo Snow Festival

Taking place annually for a week in February since 1950, the Sapporo Snow Festival is a magnificent winter celebration held in Sapporo City, the capital of Hokkaido. This renowned event showcases breathtaking snow and ice sculptures, attracting over two million visitors each year. Spanning across four sites in Sapporo—Odori Park, Tsudome, and Susukino—more than 200 sculptures, ranging from temples to beloved cartoon characters, adorn the festival grounds. The sculptures are beautifully illuminated until 10 PM every day. In addition to this visual extravaganza, attendees can enjoy various concerts and events held throughout the festival.

For the optimal vantage point to appreciate Odori Park, the festival's main location stretching 1.5 kilometers, head to the Sapporo TV Tower Observation Deck located at the eastern end of Odori Park.

How To Get To the Sapporo Snow Festival
Odori Park can be reached with ease, just a minute's walk from Odori Station or a leisurely 12-minute stroll from Sapporo Station.

2. Escape The City Life In Furano And Biei
Furano and Biei, situated in the central region of Hokkaido, are renowned tourist destinations celebrated for their awe-inspiring

natural landscapes. To witness the breathtaking beauty, plan your visit between April and October, when the hills of Shikisai-no-oka adorn themselves with a vibrant tapestry of multicolored flowers, and the lavender fields at Farm Tomita in Furano captivate the senses. At Shikisai-no-oka, you can explore the hills in a golf buggy and have the opportunity to interact with the alpacas residing on the farm. During the winter season, the farm transforms into a snow-covered wonderland, inviting visitors to enjoy exhilarating snowmobile rides.

Just outside the Shirogane Onsen hot spring resort in Biei lies the enchanting Aoiike, also known as the blue pond, boasting a striking azure hue. This man-made pond has gained popularity in recent years, with its hues varying with the changing seasons and weather conditions.

For panoramic views of the valley, take a ride on the Furano Ropeway, a gondola offering year-round access. In summer and autumn, revel in the vibrant colors of the surrounding forests and mountains as you explore the meticulously maintained hiking trails.

How To Get To Furano and Biei

If you arrive at Sapporo Airport, conveniently obtain a Furano-Biei Free Ticket from the JR counter. This ticket, priced at ¥6,500, provides round-trip transportation and unlimited free travel within the Furano and Biei area for four consecutive days. From June to August, direct JR trains run between Sapporo Station and Furano Station. To reach Biei Station, a transfer to Asahikawa Station is required. Additionally, tourist buses connect Furano, Biei, and Shirogane Blue Pond. Several sightseeing tour buses also offer direct transportation from Sapporo to Furano and Biei.

3. Check Out the Harbor City Otaru

Located just a 30-minute train ride northwest of Sapporo, Otaru is a captivating harbor city, making it an ideal day trip from Hokkaido's capital. Once a prominent trade and fishing port in the late 1800s, Otaru now charms visitors with its meticulously preserved canal area and historic buildings, once utilized by shipping and trade companies.

During the Otaru Snow Light Path Festival, held in February alongside the Sapporo Snow Festival, the city adorns itself with shimmering lanterns and delicate snow sculptures, illuminating the nights from 5 pm to 9 pm.

How To Get To Otaru
From Sapporo Station, board the JR Express Airport train to Otaru Station, a journey lasting approximately 30 minutes.

Book a Tour in Otaru
Embark on a 6-hour guided tour that covers Otaru's highlights, including the Otaru Canal, Otaru Art Base, Otaru Sakaimachi Street, Tanaka Sake Brewing Kikkogura, and Tenguyama Ropeway Ski Museum. Immerse yourself in the rich history and vibrant culture of this charming area.

4. Hit the Slopes In Niseko

Nestled southwest of Sapporo City, Niseko is widely regarded as Japan's premier ski resort, offering copious amounts of light powder snow. The prime season for powdery snow is January and February, attracting a significant number of international visitors. Beyond skiing, Niseko presents a wealth of exhilarating winter adventures, including the half-day snow view rating tour. Notably, the major resorts in Niseko, namely Grand Hirafu, Niseko Village, Hanazono, and Annupuri, are interconnected atop the mountain, facilitating seamless skiing experiences across all establishments.

Georgia Tucker

How To Get To Niseko

From December to March, multiple bus companies operate direct services between Sapporo City and Niseko. The travel time ranges from 2.5 to 4 hours, depending on the pick-up location and destination. Alternatively, renting a car provides flexibility and convenience, allowing for easy exploration of other nearby ski resorts and places of interest.

Book a Tour in Niseko:

Experience the unique activity of snow view rafting in Niseko. Accompanied by professional guides, embark on an exhilarating ride along snowy rivers, with moments of respite to enjoy a cup of warm coffee or tea amidst the crisp wintry atmosphere. This unforgettable activity comes highly recommended for those seeking a truly memorable experience.

5. Explore Matsumae: The Little Kyoto Of The North

Situated at the southernmost tip of Hokkaido, Matsumae town holds the distinction of being a former castle town and is widely regarded as the "Little Kyoto of the North." Its strategic location, a mere 20 kilometers from Aomori prefecture, attracted merchants involved in shipping trade during the Edo period.

Matsumae Castle, also known as Fukushima Castle, stands as the sole Japanese-style castle ever built in Hokkaido. The present-day castle tower, completed in the early 1960s, overlooks the vast expanse of Matsumae Park. This expansive park is adorned with over ten thousand cherry trees, delighting visitors with their blossoms each spring.

How To Get To MATSUMAE CASTLE AND MATSUMAE PARK
To reach Matsumae Castle, board the Hakodate Bus bound for Matsumae from JR Kikonai station, alighting at the Matsujo bus stop (approximately 1.5 hours). From the bus stop, it's a pleasant 7-minute stroll to the park.

Kikonai station is conveniently served by the JR Hokkaido Shinkansen and South Hokkaido Railway.

Book a tour in Matsumae
Immerse yourself in the allure of a bygone era and savor the traditional ceremonial cuisine! This set meal meticulously recreates the wedding feast of Matumae's 14th feudal lord, drawing inspiration from historical records. Through this dining experience, you can deepen your understanding of the region's history and indulge in its authentic traditional cuisine. Following the meal, a knowledgeable guide will accompany you on a tour of Matsumae Castle, Matsumae Park, and Matsumae Taramachi. Concluding the tour, you'll have the opportunity to unwind and rejuvenate in a beloved onsen hot spring.

Lord's Cuisine & Matsumae Walking Tour with Hot Spring Bathing

As the northernmost castle town in Japan, Matsumae provides an exquisite recreation of the celebratory wedding table of the Prince of the Matsumae clan, inspired by historical sources! Why not...

6. Get Your Grub On In Hakodate

Hakodate, a prominent city in northern Japan, is renowned for its Western-style architecture, delectable seafood, and savory salt ramen, among other culinary delights. Aptly dubbed the city of gourmet food, Hakodate thrives on an abundance of crab, tuna, squid, abalone, and other delicacies, owing to the region's bountiful plankton supply. A must-try dish is the kaisen-don, a delightful bowl of assorted sashimi. For a unique experience, sample the sea urchin at Uni Murakami.

While in Hakodate, take the opportunity to visit the Russian Orthodox church, and the former British Consulate, or explore the vibrant morning market offering an array of fresh produce. Additionally, a ride on the aerial gondola to the summit of Mt. Hakodate offers captivating panoramic views of the city.

Another noteworthy attraction is the Goryokaku Fort Park, showcasing the region's sakura trees, which burst into glorious bloom from the last week of April to the first week of May. For breathtaking views of the entire fort, the Goryokaku Observation Tower is an ideal vantage point.

How To Get To HAKODATE

From Sapporo Station, board the limited express Hokuto train to Hakodate (approximately 3 hours and 19 minutes).

Consider Booking a Tour in Hakodate

Embark on an unforgettable full-day private walking tour of Hakodate, immersing yourself in its most awe-inspiring highlights, including Mt. Hakodate, Onuma Quasi-National Park, Goryokaku, and more. The itinerary can be fully customized to cater to your unique preferences and interests, guaranteeing a personalized experience that will be cherished forever.

7. Head To Lake Toya

Lake Toya forms a part of the scenic Shikotsu-Toya National Park, nestled in the southern region of Hokkaido. Accessible by car, it is approximately a 1.5-hour drive from New Chitose Airport or a 2-hour drive from Sapporo. This nearly circular lake is a caldera, and its breathtaking beauty attracted the G8 Summit to its shores in 2008. Near the lake lies Mount Usu, an active volcano that last erupted in 2000. Visitors can ascend to the summit of Mount Usu via the Usuzan Ropeway. ▶Obtain e-tickets for the Mt. Usu Ropeway

Adjacent to the lake and the foot of Mount Usu, you'll find the tranquil hot spring resort of Toyako Onsen. Enjoy an overnight stay at one of the numerous hotels, stroll along the promenade adorned with foot baths (ashiyu), and delight in the nightly firework show from May to October. The promenade also serves as the departure point for scenic boat cruises on the lake. Along the lakeshore, a sculpture garden showcases 58 magnificent sculptures.

How To Get To LAKE TOYA
From Sapporo Station, take the JR Hakodate Main Line to Toya Station (approximately 2 hours). From Toya Station, a 20-minute Donan Bus ride will bring you to Toyako Onsen.

8. Go Hiking in Daisetsuzan National Park

Daisetsuzan National Park, Japan's largest national park, proudly features the majestic Daisetsuzan Mountain range. Within this range, you'll encounter Mount Asahi (2,291 meters), Hokkaido's highest peak, and Mount Kurodake (1,984 meters), easily accessible through the convenience of a ropeway and chairlift.

Nature enthusiasts often commence their hiking journeys from Mount Kurodake, serving as the gateway to the heart of the national park. Surrounding the mountain range, several hot springs await, providing a serene haven to relax and rejuvenate after exploring the captivating surroundings.

How To Get To DAISETSUZAN NATIONAL PARK
Daisetsuzan National Park can be accessed from various directions, and the most convenient way to reach and explore the park is by renting a car.

9. Relax at Noboribetsu Onsen

Noboribetsu Onsen, Hokkaido's renowned hot spring resort, offers a plethora of Japanese ryokans and hotels with luxurious hot spring baths. If you're not planning to stay overnight, many establishments also provide drop-in onsen services for day visitors.

In addition to the hot springs, the area boasts several other captivating tourist attractions, with Jigokudani, or "hell valley," being the most famous. This geothermal area showcases billowing white steam, sulfuric vapor, and other volcanic activity, serving as the primary source of the onsen in Noboribetsu.

How To Get To Noboribetsu Onsen
Convenient express buses operate from JR Sapporo Station, taking approximately one hour, as well as from New Chitose Airport, with a similar travel time, providing direct access to Noboribetsu Onsen.

10. Check Out the Beautiful Lake Mashu

Situated in the Akan Mashu National Park in eastern Hokkaido, Lake Mashu is revered as Japan's most beautiful lake. Its crystal-clear waters are renowned for their exceptional transparency, often regarded as the clearest in the world. With a depth of 212 meters, Lake Mashu is also one of Japan's deepest lakes. However, the lake's surface is frequently covered in fog, making it challenging to enjoy an unobstructed view. Yet, the weather conditions around the lake can change rapidly, and the fog may dissipate as quickly as it appears.

Observation decks positioned along the caldera rim offer breathtaking vistas of Lake Mashu and can be easily accessed by car. Additionally, a scenic hiking trail spans approximately 7 kilometers from the first observation deck to the summit of Mount Mashudake, passing through enchanting forests and grasslands. This trail presents a fantastic option for those seeking a day of hiking amidst stunning scenery.

How To Get To Lake Mashu
The most convenient way to visit Lake Mashu is by rental car, as public transportation connections are limited in the area.

11. See Some Wildlife in Shiretoko National Park

Nestled on the Shiretoko Peninsula, Shiretoko National Park stands as one of Japan's most picturesque and lesser-explored national parks. It serves as a habitat for diverse wildlife, including brown bears, deer, and foxes. The northern tip of the peninsula can only be observed from boats or accessed through multi-day trekking tours. During winter, visitors can witness drift ice floating in the Sea of Okhotsk.

Georgia Tucker

The scenic Shiretoko Five Lakes offer captivating views of land, sea, and lakes, featuring easy hiking routes suitable for visitors of all ages. Another attraction worth exploring is the whale-watching cruise, providing the opportunity to spot the 14 different species of whales that frequent the coastline.

How To Get To Shiretoko National Park
The main entry points to Shiretoko National Park are Rausu and Utoro.

Utoro can be reached via a 90-minute drive from Memanbetsu Airport or Nakashibetsu Airport or a 2-hour bus ride from Memanbetsu Airport or Abashiri.

Rausu is approximately a 1-hour drive from Nakashibetsu Airport or a 100-minute bus ride.

12. Enjoy the Cherry Blossoms At Shizunai Nijukken Road

Immerse yourself in the enchanting ambiance of Shizunai Nijukken Road, where an impressive avenue of cherry blossom trees stretches for 7 kilometers. During the Cherry Blossom Festival held in mid-May, the approximately 3,000 cherry blossom trees lining both sides of the street bloom in full splendor, attracting locals and tourists alike to stroll beneath the spectacular blossoms and savor leisurely lunches in this captivating setting.

How To Get To Shizunai Nijukken Road
From Sapporo Station, take the Hidaka Main Line to Shizunai Station, which takes approximately 2 hours. From Shizunai Station, it is a 20-minute car or taxi ride to Nijukken Road.

13. See Some Cute Animals at Asahiyama Zoo

Located in Asahikawa, Hokkaido, Asahiyama Zoo offers an excellent opportunity to spend part of the day, particularly for families on a trip. Instead of venturing into national parks in search of potentially hazardous wildlife, visiting one of Hokkaido's most popular zoos allows you to safely observe a variety of animals, including rare species such as penguins and polar bears.

14. Visit A Local Festival

As an island, Hokkaido possesses a distinct culture that sets it apart from mainland Japan. While the world-famous Sapporo

Snow Festival often comes to mind when thinking of Hokkaido, the region hosts numerous enjoyable festivals throughout the year. From vibrant flower festivals in spring to mesmerizing fireworks displays in summer and enchanting ice and snow village festivals in winter, there's always something fun and festive happening regardless of the season.

15. Have A Drink at The Sapporo Beer Museum

Hokkaido is recognized as the birthplace of beer in Japan, with Sapporo beer gaining international acclaim. The best place to savor this iconic brew is in Sapporo itself. Immerse yourself in the history, growth, and brewing process of Sapporo beer at the Sapporo Beer Museum. After exploring the museum, visitors have the opportunity to sample a variety of beers, some of which are exclusive to the museum, for a small fee. For those seeking further enjoyment, a beer garden with several restaurants is conveniently located adjacent to the museum.

HOW TO GET TO THE SAPPORO BEER MUSEUM
The museum can be accessed via the "Loop 88 Factory Line" bus, which stops at Odori Station and Seibu in front of Sapporo Station. Alternatively, it is a 25-minute walk from Sapporo Station for those who don't mind a slightly longer stroll.

THE 10 BEST HOTELS IN HOKKAIDO

Hotels and resorts in Japan offer unique and captivating experiences that often make it difficult for guests to leave their premises. One of the greatest attractions is the presence of natural onsen hot springs, which many hotels are built upon. In the enchanting and snow-covered region of Hokkaido, these onsens hold even greater allure. Additionally, Hokkaido is renowned for its ski resorts, further enhancing its reputation as a destination of choice. Hokkaido's hotels, whether situated in the city, by the lakeside, or atop mountains, epitomize the epitome of luxury, beauty, and excitement in the Japanese hotel and resort scene. Here, we present ten of the finest establishments in the region.

The Windsor Hotel Toya Resort & Spa

336 Shimizu, Toyako, Abuta District, Hokkaido 049-5722, Japan

PHONE +81 142-73-1111

Nestled on the shores of Lake Toya, one of Hokkaido's southernmost points, The Windsor Hotel Toya Resort & Spa epitomizes luxury. Its unrivaled location offers breathtaking views, complemented by exceptional dining experiences and a wide range of spa treatments. Guests staying at this lakeside hotel can enjoy a variety of activities throughout the year. During the summer, tennis, golf, horseback riding, fly fishing, and glassblowing lessons are available, while winter activities include sledding, skiing, snowboarding, and stargazing. The onsen facilities and wellness experiences, such as back and foot massages and access to the private indoor pool, provide further relaxation. The average nightly rate is $350.

Furano Hotel

Gakudensanku, 学田三区 富良野市 北海道 076-0035, Japan

PHONE +81 11-598-2828

Located in the central Hokkaido town of Furano, known as Hokkaido's "Belly Button," Furano Hotel offers a unique experience with stunning views of the summer lavender fields and winter ski resorts. Blending Eastern and Western comforts, the hotel features hot spring baths, traditional stone saunas, and a restaurant that serves exquisite French cuisine. Summer visitors can delight in the nearby lavender gardens and fields, while winter guests can take advantage of the hotel's ski storage. The average cost per night is $150.

Otaru Ryotei Kuramure

This exceptional hotel in Hokkaido emerged from the concept of repurposing and connecting traditional Japanese storehouses (kura). Several years were dedicated to designing the hotel, resulting in a cozy and secure ambiance that ensures guests' absolute comfort. Surrounded by a forest that exudes the scents of rain, grass, and falling leaves, Otaru Ryotei Kuramure offers a tranquil and picturesque environment. True to Hokkaido's hospitality, the hotel features its own private onsen hot springs. The restaurant prides itself on using fresh, locally sourced ingredients from nearby farmers and fishermen, offering guests an authentic Hokkaido culinary experience. The average nightly rate is approximately $550.

Akan Yuku no Sato Tsuruga

4-chōme-6-10 Akanchō Akankoonsen, Kushiro, Hokkaido 085-0467, Japan

PHONE +81 154-67-4000

Located on the shores of Lake Akan, Akan Yuku no Sato Tsuruga is a distinctive hotel that draws inspiration from native Ainu architecture and traditions. The hotel's name, Tsuruga, originates from the local Japanese crane, a significant figure in Ainu mythology. Guests can enjoy thirty-three separate onsen baths located across different floors, immersing themselves in the healing waters while admiring the scenic surroundings. The dining experience showcases the rich flavors of local Hokkaido cuisine, renowned throughout Japan. The hotel offers buffet-style meals and exciting multi-course dinners. Guests can also explore and appreciate the captivating views of the surrounding lake. The average cost for a stay at Akan Yuku no Sato Tsuruga is $280.

Ki Niseko

Japan, 〒044-0080 Hokkaido, Abuta District, Niseko, Nisekohirafu 1 Jō, 3-chōme– 8 Hirafu 1-jo 3-chrome 11-4 Kutchan-cho, Abuta-gun

PHONE +81 136-22-2121

Niseko is renowned for its majestic mountain range and snowy winters, with Mt. Yotei as its crown jewel. At the boutique ski hotel, Ki Niseko, guests are treated to warm hospitality and luxurious amenities befitting a ski resort. The traditional onsen hot springs, surrounded by pristine white snow, offer an unparalleled experience, especially during the peak of the ski season. The alpine spa features massages that are ideal for guests seeking relaxation after a day on the slopes. The cuisine showcases local ingredients and provides guests with exceptional traditional Hokkaido dishes. The average cost for a night at Ki Niseko is $670.

Ryotei Hanayura

Ryotei Hanayura, located in the serene Noboribetsu Hot Spring District, offers a tranquil ryokan experience with traditional rooms featuring private onsen. The rooms are furnished with comfortable futons and cozy yukata robes for guests' utmost comfort during their stay. A delightful breakfast and dinner, incorporating seasonal ingredients, are included, ensuring a nourishing and satisfying culinary experience. Alongside the private baths, the ryokan also provides larger communal baths for guests' enjoyment. Many rooms offer scenic views of the nearby lake, and the famous Hell Valley is just a 10-minute walk away. With a bus stop conveniently located in front of the hotel, exploring Noboribetsu is effortless, and the hotel staff can arrange shuttle buses to access more remote areas. With a focus on hospitality, Ryotei Hanayura aims to ensure that guests depart feeling relaxed and content. The average cost for a night at Ryotei Hanayura is $535.

MyStays Premier Sapporo Park

Japan, 〒064-0809 Hokkaido, Sapporo, Chuo Ward, Minami 9 Jōnishi, 2-chōme-2-1 0
ホテルマイステイズプレミア札幌パーク

PHONE +81 11-512-3456

Located a mere ten minutes from the main JR Sapporo train station and a two-minute walk from the expansive Nakajima Park and Nakajima Koen Subway Station, MyStays Premier Sapporo Park is an ideal hotel for a city break in Sapporo. The hotel offers a range of luxurious amenities, including natural hot spring baths, a sauna, and hot tubs, catering to guests' relaxation needs. For skiing enthusiasts, the hotel provides practical solutions such as ski storage, laundry services, and car rental. Guests can indulge in a Japanese-style breakfast or savor the international buffet. The hotel's restaurants serve farm-fresh cuisine and specialty seafood for dinner, allowing guests to experience the best of Hokkaido's dining right within the hotel. The average cost for a night at MyStays Premier Sapporo Park is $72.

Chalet Ivy

Japan, 〒044-0080 Hokkaido, Abuta District, Kutchan, Nisekohirafu 1 Jō, 3-chōme– 6 ニセコひらふ1条3丁目6-32

PHONE +81 136-22-1123

Centrally situated in Niseko, a renowned skiing area in Hokkaido, Chalet Ivy offers a convenient and picturesque location with spectacular mountain views. The hotel caters to guests' comfort with roaring fires, private hot springs, and luxurious massage services after a day on the slopes. Japanese cuisine is served in the restaurant, accompanied by a hearty breakfast and a well-curated selection of wines and sake at the bar. The hotel provides private ski lockers, ski and snowboard equipment rentals, and ski passes for guests' convenience. While the hotel is within walking distance of the first ski lift, a complimentary shuttle is available to transport guests and their equipment. Chalet Ivy is conveniently located a 15-minute drive from JR Hirafu Train Station. The average cost for a night at Chalet Ivy is $240.

Georgia Tucker

Kitayuzawa Mori No Soraniwa

For those looking to explore the scenic wonders of Shikotsu Toya National Park, Kitayuzawa Mori No Soraniwa offers the perfect location and even provides a complimentary shuttle bus service from JR Sapporo Station. The hotel seamlessly blends Japanese and Western comforts, featuring rooms with Western-style beds and tatami seating areas. The menu at the hotel's restaurant offers both Japanese and Western options for breakfast, lunch, and dinner. Guests can unwind in indoor and outdoor hot springs or enjoy swimming in the outdoor hot spring pool after a day of hiking. The hotel warmly welcomes families and organizes activities upon request, including a child-friendly buffet during dinner. The average cost for a stay at Kitayuzawa Mori No Soraniwa is $245.

La Vista Hakodate Bay

Courtesy of La Vista Hakodate Bay

12-6 Toyokawachō, Hakodate, Hokkaido 040-0065, Japan

PHONE +81 138-23-6111

Offering sweeping views of Hakodate's city and harbor, La Vista Hakodate Bay provides a luxurious retreat for guests. The hotel features relaxing rooftop hot spring baths, a spa, and a sauna. Its fine dining restaurants serve European and Chinese cuisine, while the spacious art deco rooms draw inspiration from the Taisho period. Guests can savor a Japanese buffet breakfast and enjoy in-room coffee grinders and facilities. Despite its serene ambiance, the hotel is conveniently located within a ten-minute walk from the city center, as well as a three-minute walk from the bay and Kanemori Red Brick Warehouses. The average price for a night at La Vista Hakodate Bay is $250.

15 BEST PLACES TO VISIT IN HOKKAIDO

If you are seeking a unique destination or planning an extended stay in Japan, Hokkaido should be on your travel radar. As the northernmost prefecture in Japan, Hokkaido offers vast and diverse landscapes, surpassing the combined size of the six largest prefectures. Its geographical location also results in contrasting sceneries depending on the season you choose to visit. Whether you are captivated by the winter wonderland, charmed by the blooming spring, enticed by the vibrant festivals, or enthralled by the captivating autumn colors, Hokkaido promises a memorable experience that will beckon you to return throughout the year.

New Chitose Airport

Commencing our list of recommended destinations in Hokkaido, we turn our attention to the likely point of arrival for most travelers: New Chitose Airport (新千歳空港). However, this airport transcends its role as a mere transportation hub, offering visitors a plethora of shopping, dining, and leisure options. Within the airport, a wide array of shops, restaurants, and cafes present Hokkaido's renowned culinary delights. Furthermore, a short ten-minute shuttle bus ride away lies "RERA," a sizable outlet mall providing opportunities for clothing, footwear, outdoor equipment, and more. Remarkably, flight schedules are displayed within the mall, allowing travelers to conveniently explore before embarking on their return journey home.

Muroran

Next on our itinerary, we encounter Muroran (室蘭), a significant port city facilitating the vital connection between Hokkaido and Honshu, Japan's main island. As a consequence, numerous companies have established factories and warehouses near the port, creating a distinctive industrial ambiance that has captivated many, particularly photographers, who appreciate this unique setting. The nocturnal scenery, in particular, garners significant attention, to the extent that boat tours have been organized for visitors to witness the city's most photogenic facets. Additionally, Muroran boasts Cape Chikiu, a picturesque location affording breathtaking views of the Pacific Ocean, especially during sunrise.

official website: https://muro-kanko.com

Cape Soya

Continuing our exploration, we recommend a visit to Cape Soya (宗谷岬), situated at latitude 45°31'N and officially recognized as the northernmost point of Japan. Symbolized by a monument resembling the northern star, this location offers visitors the opportunity to acquire a certificate commemorating their arrival at this point, serving as a remarkable souvenir and a captivating anecdote. From Cape Soya, glimpses of Sakhalin Island (Russia) can be observed. Found in the town of Wakkanai (稚内), this destination also entices visitors to discover the enchanting Shiroimichi (白い道), an 11-kilometer-long white path that has gained popularity in recent years due to its photogenic allure. Additionally, savoring Takoshabu, an octopus shabu-shabu dish, is highly recommended.

official website: https://www.north-hokkaido.com/spot/detail_1018.html

Otaru

Otaru City (小樽市) represents another historically significant port city that has masterfully preserved its distinctive urban landscape, making it a delightful destination for travelers. During its flourishing period, a canal measuring over one kilometer in length was constructed to facilitate transportation, which has now evolved into a captivating tourist attraction. Alongside the canal, numerous buildings and warehouses have been repurposed into restaurants and shops, enhancing the city's allure. A visit to Otaru should also include a stop at the Nikka Yoichi whisky distillery, where a captivating whisky-making experience awaits.

official website: https://otaru.gr.jp/

Lake Akan

Situated on the eastern side of Hokkaido, Lake Akan (阿寒湖) is a caldera lake renowned for its association with Marimo, a unique type of green algae that assumes various captivating shapes, most notably round. Recognized as a special national natural treasure, Marimo attracts considerable attention. The lake also serves as a popular fishing spot for Himemasu and Ito, both types of trout. Adjacent to the lake lies Akanko Onsen (阿寒湖温泉), a renowned hot spring destination, complemented by a significant Ainu community. Visitors have the opportunity to immerse themselves in Ainu culture and savor traditional Ainu cuisine.

official website: https://en.kushiro-lakeakan.com/

Tokachi Ranch

Nestled amidst the expansive plains of central Hokkaido, Tokachi Ranch (十勝牧場) stands as another enticing destination worthy of consideration. Encompassing a vast expanse of 4,100 hectares, this ranch boasts two rivers, an observatory providing unobstructed vistas of the magnificent scenery and galloping horses, and a myriad of diverse animals, including horses, sheep, and cows. Notably, a popular attraction within the ranch is a 1.3-kilometer-long path lined with birch trees, renowned for its appearances in Japanese television series and commercials, making it an in-demand spot for capturing memorable photographs.

website:
http://www.nlbc.go.jp/tokachi/bokujougaiyou/kankouspot/

Lake Toya

Lake Toya, situated in the southwest region of Hokkaido, is a prominent donut-shaped lake that owes its formation to a volcanic eruption approximately 110,000 years ago. Renowned for its abundant hot springs, Toyako Onsen stands out as one of Hokkaido's most popular onsen towns. From mid-April to October, visitors can enjoy nightly fireworks displays over the lake. Additionally, the island at the center of Lake Toya offers a popular hiking trail where one may encounter over 100 Ezoshika, a species of deer.

Patchwork Road

The Patchwork Road, located near Biei Town in central Hokkaido, stretches between national highways 237 and 252. This scenic route traverses expansive fields showcasing a vibrant mosaic of different flowers and crops, resembling a magnificent patchwork. The interplay of colors and winding paths creates a visually captivating landscape.

Unkai Terrace

Situated at an elevation of 1,080 meters, Unkai Terrace serves as an observatory spot where visitors have the chance to witness the Unkai, a mesmerizing sea of clouds that blankets the area below. While the sighting of this natural phenomenon is not guaranteed for all, the terrace provides a breathtaking 210-degree panoramic view of the central region of Hokkaido. Operated by Hoshino Resorts, Unkai Terrace offers various amenities such as seating areas, hammocks, and a café. The site is open between May and October and transforms into a popular ski resort during winter.

official website (summer): https://www.snowtomamu.jp/summer/

official website (winter): https://www.snowtomamu.jp/winter/en/

Shiretoko National Park
Included in our list of Hokkaido's must-visit destinations is Shiretoko National Park, a UNESCO World Heritage site located on the Shiretoko Peninsula in the easternmost part of Hokkaido. Nature enthusiasts, animal lovers, and those seeking awe-inspiring vistas will find this park a captivating destination. Covering an area of approximately 61 hectares, the park boasts attractions such as the renowned Shiretoko Goko Lakes, natural hot springs, enchanting waterfalls, and numerous other breathtaking natural wonders.

Georgia Tucker

Blue Pond

The Blue Pond, situated on the outskirts of Biei town, has gained popularity due to its inclusion as a wallpaper selection on MacBook Pro computers. The vivid blue hue of the pond results from a chemical reaction, with the shade varying according to weather conditions. This location is conveniently located near Furano, another popular town in Hokkaido, making it a worthy addition to your itinerary if you are visiting either Furano or Biei.

Georgia Tucker

official website: https://www.biei-hokkaido.jp/en/

Noboribetsu Onsen

Among the many renowned onsen spots in Hokkaido, Noboribetsu Onsen stands out as the most popular. This onsen area offers nine distinct types of natural hot springs, each believed to provide unique health benefits. Within the Noboribetsu area, visitors can also explore the Noboribetsu Jigokudani, a crater with a diameter of 450 meters, formed by the eruption of Mt. Hiyori. These attractions are encompassed within the Shikotsu-Toya National Park, and nearby, a bear farm offers an additional point of interest.

Hakodate

Hakodate City, one of Hokkaido's largest cities, is situated on the southern coast, just across the Tsugaru Strait from Aomori Prefecture. Boasting a wide array of attractions, Hakodate entices visitors with its culinary delights, historical sites, observatories, and exceptional onsen facilities. The night view from Mt. Hakodate, which can be reached by ropeway, is renowned as one of the finest in Japan, further enhancing the city's appeal.

Niseko

Niseko is renowned for its exceptional ski resort, attracting ski and snowboard enthusiasts from around the world. Not only does Niseko offer accessibility and excellent mountain conditions, but it also features numerous onsen sources—15 in total—providing a rejuvenating experience for visitors. However, Niseko's appeal extends beyond winter, as it provides a beautiful natural setting for outdoor activities such as canoeing and trekking during other seasons.

Sapporo

Lastly, we have Sapporo City, the largest city in Hokkaido, which serves as a gateway for travelers arriving at New Chitose Airport. This vibrant city offers an abundance of attractions, including historical sites such as the Sapporo Clock Tower, the Sapporo TV Tower, and the Former Hokkaido Government Office. Furthermore, Susukino, the largest red-light district in Hokkaido, adds to the city's allure. The Sapporo Snow Festival, a prominent winter event, is not to be missed by those visiting during the winter season.

Georgia Tucker

20 RESTAURANTS IN HOKKAIDO TO TRY ITS MANY DELICACIES

Blessed by its favorable climate and abundant natural resources, Hokkaido boasts a diverse array of delicacies that can be savored throughout the year. From fresh seafood such as crabs and sea urchin (Uni) to premium meats like Jingisukan (Mongolian Mutton Barbecue) and Tokachi pork, as well as iconic dishes like miso ramen and soup curry, the culinary options are truly captivating. In this guide, we present a selection of highly recommended restaurants in Sapporo, Otaru, Hakodate, and other locations across Hokkaido. Before embarking on your travels, explore this list to ensure an exceptional gourmet experience in Hokkaido.

For a comprehensive list of Japanese cuisine restaurants in and around Hokkaido, please refer to our full listings.

1.[Genghis Khan (Grilled Mutton)] Genghis Khan Hitsujikai No Mise "Itadakimasu"

At Genghis Khan Hitsujikai no Mise "Itadakimasu," we specialize in serving grilled mutton dishes made from lamb aged between 10 and 16 months. This age range ensures that the lamb meat is at its peak richness and flavor, surpassing traditional mutton. Our specially bred animals combine an English strain with a fine-textured and tender meat strain, resulting in premium meat that is available in limited quantities in Japan. By sourcing the meat from our in-house farms, we can offer it at a reasonable price.

Our dedicated team is committed to providing exceptional service, ensuring that your dining experience is both memorable and enjoyable. Whether you are visiting for business or leisure, we invite all enthusiasts of the Genghis Khan grilled mutton dish to savor our rendition of this local Hokkaido delicacy. Private rooms are also available for business meetings or entertainment purposes.

Details:

Opening hours: [Weekdays, Saturday, Day Before Holidays] 11:30 - 03:00 / [Sunday, Holidays] 11:30 - 23:00

Closed: None

Average price: [Dinner] 3,000 JPY

Access: A 2-minute walk from Namboku Subway Line, Susukino station.

Address: 5-1-6 Minami Gojonishi, Chuo-ku, Sapporo, Hokkaido

2. [Donburi] Hakodate Asaichi Aji No Ichiban

With 34 years of experience in Hakodate, Hakodate Asaichi Aji no Ichiban is renowned for serving dishes made with the freshest seafood available from the nearby market. Our extensive menu offers over 50 items, including ramen, set meals, and donburi (rice-based dishes). Whether it's the summer season or winter, we ensure that our customers enjoy the finest seafood delicacies prepared with utmost care.

Georgia Tucker

Details:

Opening hours: May - October 6:30 am - 3:00 pm / November - April 7:00 am - 2:00 pm

Closed: None

Average price: [Dinner] 1,300 JPY

Access: Exit JR Hakodate Station and head right toward Hakodate Asaichi market. The restaurant is located across from Donburi Yokocho market.

Address: 11-13 Wakamatsu-cho, Hakodate, Hokkaido

3. [Sashimi (Raw Fish)] Nizakana Sashimi Shunsai Uminoshiki

Indulge in the exquisite flavors of Nizakana Sashimi Shunsai Uminoshiki, where our signature dish, "Savory Egg Custard with

Crab Soup Stock," awaits. This delectable creation combines a rich egg custard base with a medley of luxurious seasonal seafood such as sea urchins and thornyhead rockfish. The dish features the renowned "Sapporo Yellow" onion, enhancing its sweetness, along with the distinct umami-filled flavors of Nemuro crab miso-paste soup stock. To ensure the utmost freshness, we keep live crab, botan shrimp, and other seafood in our restaurant's tank, preparing them upon order. Our commitment to quality extends to sourcing the finest seasonal ingredients directly from local markets and fishing harbors, presented with meticulous attention to aesthetic plate arrangements. Occasionally, we feature fish caught by our own hands, adding a special touch to the menu. We warmly invite you to inquire about the catch of the day, as we strive to foster a heartfelt connection between our cuisine and our guests' dining experience.

Details:

Opening hours: 18:00 - 02:00

Closed: Sundays

Average price: [Dinner] 6,300 JPY

Access: A 3-minute walk from Susukino station on the Nanboku subway line.

Address: G4 Bldg.6F, Minami Rokujo Nishi 4chome, Chuo-ku, Sapporo-shi, Hokkaido

4. [Soup Curry] Soup Curry Shabazo (Odori / Soup Curry)

Distinguished for its use of meticulously boiled lamb stock, Soup Curry Shabazo offers an array of creatively crafted soup curry dishes in Hokkaido. The restaurant provides a spacious interior with options for counter seating and private rooms, creating an inviting ambiance for diners to relax and savor their meals. Noteworthy among their offerings is the must-try Lamb-burg soup curry, available with a choice of 9 or 15 vegetables. For lamb enthusiasts, this dish is a true delight. Customers can select their preferred soup stock from options such as spiced lamb bone soup, healthy fish soup, beef bone, tomato soup, or a combination of beef and lamb. Furthermore, the level of spiciness can be tailored to individual preferences, with 7 distinct spice levels to choose from.

Details:

Opening hours: [Weekdays, Saturday] Lunch 11:30 am - 3:00 pm (L.O. 2:30 pm), Dinner 5:00 pm - 10:00 pm (L.O. [Food] 9:00 pm [Drink], 9:30 pm) *Lunch and dinner service ends when soup runs out.

Closed: Sunday, National Holidays, Golden Week (5/3 - 5/7), Obon (8/11 - 8/16), Beginning and end of the year

Average price: [Dinner] 1,200 JPY / [Lunch] 1,200 JPY

Access: Subway Odori Station, next to Sapporo Eki-mae underground walkway Exit 10. Located near the Sapporo North Plaza entrance.

Address: B1, Sapporo North Plaza, 4, Kitaichijo Nishi, Chuo-ku, Sapporo-shi, Hokkaido

5. [Japanese Cuisine] Japanese Cuisine Matsumae

Japanese Cuisine Matsumae offers a refined dining experience, presenting delicate arrangements and unique flavors that are characteristic of exquisite Japanese cuisine. The master chef carefully selects fresh seasonal ingredients to ensure the highest quality. Whether you seek a casual solo meal at the counter seats, a gathering with family and friends, or a private setting to entertain clients, we invite you to visit Japanese Cuisine Matsumae.

Details:

Open: Lunch 11:30 am - 3:00 pm (Last Order 2:30 pm) / Dinner 5:00 pm - 9:00 pm (Last Order 8:30 pm)

Closed: None

Average Price: Dinner - 6,000 JPY / Lunch - 2,000 JPY

Access: Take the city tram line and alight at Shiyakushomae Station or Uoihchiba-dori Station. Head towards Hakodate Port, and you will find us on the second floor of the East Building of the Hakodate Kokusai Hotel.

Address: 2F, East Bldg., Hakodate Kokusai Hotel, 5-10, Otemachi, Hakodate-shi, Hokkaido

6. [Sushi] Otaru Masazushi Main Branch (Otaru / Sushi)

Established for 70 years, Otaru Masazushi Main Branch proudly holds its ground in the fiercely competitive sushi scene of Otaru. The first floor offers counter tables, while the second floor provides both table seats and traditional tatami rooms. Every ingredient is meticulously chosen, with a particular emphasis on the selection of world-class Atlantic tuna weighing over 300 kilograms, sourced from the southeastern coast of Canada. We highly recommend their renowned "Masazushi - Takumi" (5,800 JPY), an assortment of Hokkaido's seasonal specialties.

Details:

Open: Monday, Tuesday, Thursday - Sunday, Holidays, Day Before Holidays: 11:00 am - 10:00 pm

Closed: Wednesday

Average Price: Dinner - 3,500 JPY

Access: Alight at JR Otaru Station and take a 3 to 4-minute taxi ride to reach us.

Address: 1-1-1 Hanazono, Otaru, Hokkaido [Map]

7. [Uni] Uni Murakami Hakodate Main Branch (Hakodate / Japanese Cuisine)

Uni Murakami Hakodate Main Branch has been serving top-quality, additive-free fresh sea urchins for 60 years. Located in Hakodate's bustling market area, it is a popular destination where queues are a common sight on weekends. Their "Additive-free fresh uni rice bowl" (4,000 JPY, excluding tax) and "House-made uni gratin" (850 JPY, excluding tax) highlight the rich sweetness of uni, harmoniously complemented by their special soy sauce. With a keen focus on pairing flavors, the restaurant offers seven Hokkaido-centered Japanese sake selections that enhance the uni experience, along with a seasonal "3 sake sampling set."

Details:

Open: Weekdays except Wednesday, Weekends, National Holidays, Day before National Holidays: Lunch - 8:30 am to 2:30 pm (Last Order 2:00 pm) (November to mid-April: 9:00 am to 2:30 pm (Last Order 2:00 pm)), Dinner - 5:00 pm to 10:00 pm (Last Order 9:00 pm)

Closed: Wednesday

Average Price: Dinner - 5,000 JPY / Lunch - 3,800 JPY

Access: A 5-minute walk from JR Hakodate Station, situated at the back of the Hakodate Morning Market.

Address: 22-1, Otemachi, Hakodate, Hokkaido [Map]

8. [Kaisen-Don] Kita No Donburiya Takinami Shokudo (Otaru / Kaisen-Don)

Kita no Donburiya Takinami Shokudo is nestled within the market near Otaru Station. Their signature dish, the "Original Wagamama-don" (1,800 JPY plus tax), allows you to personalize your kaisen-don by choosing three to four seafood ingredients from a selection of over ten options, including ikura (salmon roe) and raw uni (sea urchin). You can also customize the rice portion to create a unique rice bowl dish with seafood. Pair it with

Hokkaido's exclusive "Sapporo Classic Beer" or one of the many local liquors available.

Details:

Open: 8:00 am - 5:00 pm

Closed: None

Average Price: Dinner - 1,500 JPY

Access: Located within the "Otaru Triangle Market," just outside Otaru Station.

Address: Sankaku Ichiba-nai, 3-10-16 Inaho, Otaru, Hokkaido

9. [Yakitori] Yakitori No Ippei Main Store

Originating in the industrial area of Muroran City, Muroran Yakitori was born out of the desire to cater to hard-working laborers. Renowned for its distinct combination of onions, pork, and Western-style karashi mustard, this style of yakitori has gained recognition. Our premium pork yakitori is made exclusively with the freshest Hokkaido meat, while our succulent and tender tsukune yakitori is crafted using a special blend of chicken and pork, enhanced by a signature dipping sauce of egg yolks and karashi mustard. At Yakitori no Ippei Main Store, we provide a romantic and relaxing ambiance suitable for a diverse range of diners, including businessmen, families with young children, and couples of all ages. The atmosphere is lively yet laid-back.

Georgia Tucker

Details:

Open: Monday - Thursday: 5:00 pm - 11:00 pm, Friday/Saturday/Eve of National Holiday: 5:00 pm - 12:00 am, Sunday: 5:00 pm - 10:00 pm

Closed: None

Average Price: Dinner - 2,000 JPY

Access: A ten-minute walk from the West Exit of Higashi-Muroran Station. Pass through Nakajima, and you will find us at the rear of Nagasakiya, facing the highway.

Address: 1-17-3 Nakajima-cho, Muroran-shi, Hokkaido

10. [Squid] Ikasei Main Branch (Chuobyoin-Mae / Izakaya (Japanese Pub))

"Squid Ikasei Main Branch" is a distinguished izakaya in Hakodate that specializes in serving generous portions of the region's specialty squid. Our culinary offerings are guaranteed to satisfy seafood enthusiasts with their fresh and delectable squid preparations. When an order is placed, we carefully select one of the morning's catches from our tank to ensure unparalleled freshness. Our exclusive live squid, available from January to May as a seasonal delicacy, captivates diners with its unmatched sweetness and texture. Additionally, our popular Ikasei fry, a delectable combination of minced squid, shrimp, and vegetables, is a highly recommended option. As you dine, don't miss the opportunity to explore our extensive collection of over 30 Hokkaido-centered Japanese sake brands.

Details:

Opening hours: [Weekdays, Saturdays, Days before National Holidays] 5:00 pm - 0:00 am (Last order 11:30 pm) [Sunday, National Holidays] 4:00 pm - 11:00 pm (Last order 10:30 pm)

Closed: None

Average price: [Dinner] 4,500 JPY

Access: Located just steps away from Chuobyouinmae station, Hakodate City Tram.

Address: 2-14, Honcho, Hakodate, Hokkaido

11. [Grilled Seafood] Hamaichiban (Sapporo / Japanese Cuisine)

Experience the authentic flavors of Hokkaido's seafood at Hamaichiban, a renowned restaurant that sources its fish directly from Nemuro's local fish market. The rustic wood-themed interior, featuring counter seating surrounding a hearth, creates an inviting atmosphere for diners. Our skilled chefs skillfully grill Hokkaido's fresh scallops, live uni, crabs, oysters, and various other seafood directly on the hearth, allowing you to savor the natural flavors of each ingredient. Don't miss the opportunity to try our must-try dishes, including the exquisite Live scallop from eastern Hokkaido and the flavorful Oyster.

Details:
Opening hours: Normal hours: 17:00-23:00

Closed: None

Average price: [Dinner] 3,500 JPY

Access: Located at Exit 13, Sapporo JR/Subway Station

Address: Astoria Sapporo 2F, Kita Sanjo Nishi 2chome, Chuo-ku, Sapporo-shi, Hokkaido

12. [Seafood] Sushi Yoshi (Otaru / Sushi)

At Sushi Yoshi, our skilled chef, leveraging his experience as a fisherman, meticulously selects the finest seafood to create authentic and delectable sushi. Our specialty lies in offering luxurious seafood delicacies, such as the indulgent Otaru Roman Course, which includes grilled red king crab, sushi, and sashimi, as well as the enticing Live-Grilled Yezo Abalone (market value). A favorite among locals and avid seafood connoisseurs, our restaurant is a must-visit destination for those seeking an authentic taste of Hokkaido's seafood cuisine.

Details:

Opening hours: Normal hours: 11:00 am - 10:00 pm (Last order 9:00 pm). If you plan to arrive after 9:00 pm, please contact us in advance, and we will do our best to accommodate you.

Closed: None

Average price: [Dinner] 2,500 JPY / [Lunch] 2,500 JPY

Access: A ten-minute walk from JR Otaru Station.

Address: 1-10-9 Ironai, Otaru-shi, Hokkaido

13. [Tempura] Tempura Ryori Sakura (Kushiro / Tempura)

Tempura Ryori Sakura is a renowned restaurant that excels in the art of preparing delicious tempura, a classic dish in Japanese cuisine where seafood or vegetables are delicately coated in a batter made from flour and water, then deep-fried to perfection. Our skilled chef, who also happens to be the owner, personally ventures into the mountains every morning to harvest wild plants and embarks on fishing trips to procure the freshest seasonal fish. The tempura is fried using white sesame oil, resulting in a light and delightful texture that won't weigh you down. Pair your tempura with our flavorful katsuo-flavored tentsuyu sauce for a heavenly dining experience. Among our menu highlights is the Tempura Mentaiko, featuring mentaiko (walleye pollack roe) wrapped in shiso (perilla) leaves, and the Seasonal Tempura 7-Kind Assortment, showcasing a variety of seasonal ingredients.

Details:
Tempura Ryori Sakura

Opening hours: [Weekdays, Saturday] 5:00 pm - (Last order 11:00 pm)

Closed: Sunday

Average price: [Dinner] 6,000 JPY

Access: We recommend taking a taxi from Kushiro Station. Look out for the sign of the south entrance of Eirakugai.

Address: South Entrance of Eirakugai, 3-2-12, Sakaemachi, Kushiro, Hokkaido

14. [Teppanyaki] Steak Kaisen Teppanyaki Kitakaze (Goryokaku-Koen-Mae / Teppanyaki)

At Steak Kaisen Teppanyaki Kitakaze, patrons can indulge in authentic teppanyaki cuisine, where ingredients are skillfully grilled on an iron griddle, accompanied by a selection of fine wines. The menu features a wide array of delicacies that showcase the unique qualities of each ingredient. For instance, the Fresh Abalone in a Liver-Butter Sauce (3,000 JPY) highlights abalone sourced from the sea near Hakodate, while the Sirloin (4,000 JPY) and Fillet (4,000 JPY) of Jersey beef are directly supplied from the ranch. Complementing the teppanyaki experience, the restaurant offers an extensive collection of 50 different wine bottles for guests to choose from.

Details:
Open: 6:00 pm - 11:30 pm (last order)

Closed: None

Average Price: Dinner - 7,000 JPY

Access: A 15-minute drive from JR Hakodate Station or a 2-minute walk from Goryokaku Koen Station on the streetcar line. From the Honcho intersection 6, head north on route 571 for approximately 100 meters. The restaurant will be on your left.

Address: 5F Mitsuwa Building, 8-20 Honcho, Hakodate, Hokkaido

15. [Tokachi Pork Rice Bowl] Tokachi-Butadon Ippin Kita 10 Jo Branch (Kita 13 Jo Higashi / Japanese Cuisine)

At the Kita 10 Jo branch of Tokachi-butadon Ippin, visitors to Sapporo can savor the renowned Obihiro-style pork rice bowl. Carefully selected, high-quality pork loins are sourced daily and individually charcoal grilled to order. The signature Pork Rice Bowl (714 JPY) is a culinary masterpiece. Additionally, guests should not miss the weekday-only Pork Rice Bowl Set (924 JPY), which includes a bowl of miso soup and salad, and the Pork Soup (210 JPY) while supplies last.

Georgia Tucker

Details:

Open: Weekdays, Saturday, Sunday - 11:00 am to 11:00 pm

Closed: None

Average Price: 800 JPY

Access: A 6-minute walk from Kita 13 Jo Higashi Station

Address: 4-1-21 Kitakyujo Higashi, Higashi-ku, Sapporo-shi, Hokkaido

16. [Miso Ramen] Sapporo Ichiryuan (Sapporo / Ramen)

Situated just a 2-minute walk from Sapporo Station, Sapporo Ichiryuan is a popular destination among tourists, acclaimed for its usage of local Hokkaido ingredients and homemade noodles. Among their recommended dishes are the Genki Miso Ramen

(900 JPY), renowned for its ability to bring out the nutritional benefits of garlic while eliminating its strong aroma, the simple yet satisfying Miso Ramen (780 JPY), and the indulgent Grilled Pork Miso Ramen (1,380 JPY) topped with a thick and juicy slice of grilled pork chuck.

Details:

Open: Weekdays - Lunch 11:00 am to 3:00 pm (Last Order 2:45 pm), Dinner 5:00 pm to 9:00 pm (Last Order 8:45 pm)

Closed: Irregular

September Operating Times: Closed on the 1st and 8th. Open on the 15th, 22nd, and 29th from 12:00 pm to 6:00 pm.

Average Price: 1,000 JPY

Access: Located next to Exit 23 of Sapporo Municipal Subway Station

Address: B1, Hokuren Building, 1-1 Kitayonjo Nishi, Chuo-ku, Sapporo-shi,

Source: Information available in Traditional Chinese only

Japanese Cuisine Matsumae (Hakodate/Japanese Cuisine)

17. [Kaiseki] Japanese Cuisine Matsumae (Hakodate / Japanese Cuisine)

Kaiseki refers to a meticulously crafted multi-course meal served to guests during banquets, accompanied by alcoholic beverages. Nestled within the Hakodate Kokusai Hotel, Japanese Cuisine Matsumae presents an authentic dining experience focused on

Japanese and kaiseki cuisine. The restaurant exudes a tranquil ambiance reminiscent of a hotel lounge. The highly recommended Matsumae Kaiseki (7,650 JPY) features seasonal ingredients predominantly sourced from Hakodate, beautifully arranged to create an exquisite array of delicacies. Guests can also explore the à la carte options, such as the Five-Assorted Sashimi of the Day (2,750 JPY), and indulge in Japanese sake that harmonizes perfectly with the flavors of Japanese cuisine.

Details:

Open: Lunch 11:30 am - 3:00 pm (Last Order 2:30 pm), Dinner 5:00 pm - 9:00 pm (Last Order 8:30 pm)

Closed: None

Average Price: Dinner - 6,000 JPY, Lunch - 2,000 JPY

Access: Get off at Shiyakushomae Station or Uoihchiba-dori Station on the city tram line and head towards Hakodate Port. The restaurant is located on the second floor of the East Building of the Hakodate Kokusai Hotel.

Address: 2F, East Building, Hakodate Kokusai Hotel, 5-10 Otemachi, Hakodate-shi, Hokkaido

18. [Seafood Hot Pot] Washokudokoro Unkai (Sapporo / Japanese Cuisine)

Washokudokoro Unkai, located within the ANA Crowne Plaza Hotel Sapporo, is an esteemed Japanese restaurant offering a refined dining experience. Their Hokkaido Kaiseki menu showcases the region's finest ingredients, allowing guests to indulge in seasonal dishes such as crab delicacies during the summer and fall, and comforting seafood hot pot during the colder winter months. Complementing the culinary delights, the restaurant's Japanese modern interior and attentive staff adorned in kimono create an inviting ambiance.

Details:
Opening hours:

[Lunch - Weekdays] 11:30 am - 2:00 pm (Last order 1:30 pm)

[Lunch - Saturday, Sunday, National Holidays] 11:30 am - 3:00 pm (Last order 2:30 pm)

[Dinner] 5:00 pm - 10:00 pm (Last order 9:30 pm)

Closed: None

Average price: [Dinner] 6,500 JPY / [Lunch] 2,000 JPY

Access: A 7-minute walk from Sapporo Station (JR Line) or a 2-minute walk from Sapporo Station (Toho Subway Line). Located on B1F of ANA Crowne Plaza Hotel Sapporo.

Address: B1F, ANA Crowne Plaza Hotel Sapporo, 1-2-9 Kita 3-jo Nishi, Chuo-ku, Sapporo-shi, Hokkaido

19. [Sukiyaki] An No Ie (Nakajima Koen / Shabu-Shabu, Sukiyaki)

An no Ie has been serving exquisite Wagyu shabu-shabu and sukiyaki since its establishment 30 years ago. Renowned among locals, this restaurant is often considered the benchmark for savoring exceptional Wagyu beef. Indulge in their Sukiyaki dish, where the premium soy sauce-based broth, sourced from Shikoku, enhances the umami flavors of the tender meat. Prices for Sukiyaki start from 4,200 JPY per serving.

Georgia Tucker

Details:

Opening hours: [Weekdays] Lunch 11:30 am - 2:00 pm, Dinner 5:00 pm - 11:00 pm (Last order 10:00 pm)

[Weekends, Holidays] Dinner 5:00 pm - 11:00 pm (Last order 10:00 pm)

Closed: None

Average price: [Dinner] 5,500 JPY

Access: A 5-minute walk from Nakajima-Koen Station. Adjacent to Novotel Sapporo.

Address: 6-3-15 Minami 10-jo Nishi, Chuo-ku, Sapporo, Hokkaido

20. [Sashimi] Kaisenya Hakodate Main Branch (Susukino / Izakaya)

Kaisenya Hakodate Main Branch offers an impressive selection of fresh and reasonably priced seafood. Carefully sourced from Hokkaido's bountiful waters, their offerings include live fish and other delicacies that vary according to the region and season. The Hakodate Platter, a must-try dish priced at 3,980 JPY, features a stunning arrangement of nine items, including abalone and fresh uni, beautifully presented in a hand-carved artisan ice bowl. Alternatively, indulge in unique delicacies like the Dancing Live Squid Sashimi (starting from 1,800 JPY), featuring a whole fresh raw squid caught in the morning, or the renowned Kaisen Hamayaki, where you can grill the freshest seafood yourself. A dining experience at Kaisenya Hakodate Main Branch promises to create lasting memories.

Details:

Opening hours: 5:00 pm - 11:30 pm (Last order for food at 10:30 pm, drinks at 11:00 pm)

Closed: None

Average price: [Dinner] 5,000 JPY

Access: A 3-minute walk from Susukino Station (Namboku subway line).

Address: Dai-ichi Seijusha Building, Minami 7 Jo Nishi 3-chome, Chuo-ku, Sapporo, Hokkaido

Georgia Tucker

From fresh seafood delicacies like uni and crab to Jingisukan and curry soup, these recommended restaurants in Hokkaido offer a diverse and enticing culinary experience. We hope this guide enhances your journey through Hokkaido, Japan's gourmet hotspot!

Georgia Tucker

CHAPTER EIGHT

ACCOMMODATION IN JAPAN

THE 15 BEST HOTELS IN JAPAN

Discover ancient traditions and indulge in contemporary comforts at Japan's top-notch hotels.

From the towering skyscrapers of Tokyo and the traditional ryokans of Kyoto to the pristine beaches of Okinawa and the exhilarating ski slopes of Hokkaido, Japan offers an incredibly diverse range of experiences. This diversity is reflected in the country's hotels, with some of the world's most luxurious, distinctive, and captivating properties found within Nippon.

No matter the purpose of your visit, whether you're seeking the beauty of cherry blossoms, attending a thrilling sumo wrestling match, or exploring local food markets for delectable sushi, Japan offers a hotel perfectly suited to your needs. Moreover, many of these hotels are destinations in themselves, boasting a rich history, unique traditions, luxurious amenities like onsen (hot springs) and waterfalls, or intriguing features like capsule rooms and on-site libraries. Without further delay, here are 15 remarkable hotels in Japan that cater to all budgets and occasions.

Ritz-Carlton, Kyoto

Perfectly situated in the heart of Kyoto along the Kamogawa River, with stunning views of the Higashiyama mountains, this modern yet traditionally inspired luxurious hotel exudes serene individuality. Immerse yourself in its tranquil ambiance, highlighted by a magnificent waterfall in the lobby, Zen gardens, wooden partitions, and traditional paper artworks. The Ritz-Carlton, Kyoto evokes the elegance of a luxury ryokan and offers spacious and minimalist rooms. Dining options include a high-end Japanese restaurant, an Italian eatery, and a delightful patisserie.

The Gate Hotel Kaminarimon, Tokyo

Located in the captivating Asakusa entertainment district near Tokyo's oldest temple complex, Sensoji, The Gate Hotel Kaminarimon is an excellent choice for those seeking affordable accommodation. This boutique design hotel offers a subdued interior design, complemented by attentive staff members who ensure a memorable stay. The rooms, though compact, are impeccably clean and feature neutral tones and decor that allow the city views to take center stage. Guests can savor French fusion cuisine at the on-site restaurant and enjoy the bar and terrace facilities.

Four Seasons, Kyoto

Immerse yourself in the refined elegance of this distinguished, opulent hotel, where captivating exteriors embrace captivating features such as a picturesque pond garden adorned with a traditional tea house, resplendent maple trees, cherry blossom displays, and graceful stone bridges. The enchanting allure continues within the interiors, commencing with the grand marble and cypress wood lobby adorned with delicate paper lanterns and blossoms. A seamless fusion of traditional Japanese elements and contemporary design characterizes the 123 alluring rooms, complemented by sleek, expansive bathrooms. Indulge in rejuvenating Japanese wellness rituals at the spa, or take pleasure in the tastefully designed pool. The brasserie presents an exquisite fusion of Asian and European cuisines, while a dedicated sushi bar adds to the culinary delights.

Hoshinoya, Tokyo

When in Japan, why settle for an unremarkable Western-style hotel? This extraordinary luxury ryokan seamlessly blends the old and the new, offering an authentic Japanese experience within a captivating 17-story tower. Embrace the Japanese way as you remove your shoes and step onto the tatami mat floors, and unwind in comfortably appointed futon-style beds. The ambiance is suitably tranquil, with staff dressed in traditional kimono attending to guests in the serene Ochanoma lounges, the onsen baths, and the restaurant that serves traditional Japanese breakfasts. The hotel occasionally hosts traditional performances, enhancing cultural immersion.

Georgia Tucker

Book and Bed, Tokyo

For those seeking budget-friendly accommodations, this hotel composed of wooden "capsules" in various sizes is an ideal choice. Who needs a Corby trouser press or a minibar when simplicity is the focus? Located in the vibrant Ikebukuro district adorned with vibrant neon lights, each capsule provides rows of books on one side and a curtain for privacy on the other. While there is no on-site restaurant or café, nearby dining options abound should the on-site vending machine not meet your needs. The communal bathrooms are impeccably maintained and boast modern amenities.

Georgia Tucker

Iraph Sui, Miyako Okinawa

Transport yourself to the serene paradise of Okinawa, which feels worlds apart from the rest of Japan due to its distance of 400 miles from the mainland. Embracing its idyllic surroundings, Iraph Sui on Miyako Island offers captivating rooms with awe-inspiring ocean views and balconies, creating an atmosphere of tranquility. The spectacular outdoor pool further enhances the tropical retreat experience.

Aman Tokyo

Nestled within the bustling business district of Otemachi, Aman Tokyo impresses with its exceptionally spacious 84 rooms and suites. Occupying the upper floors of a skyscraper, each abode offers magnificent vistas of the cityscape, including the Imperial Palace, Shinjuku office towers, and, on clear days, the majestic Mount Fuji. Adorned with a minimalist aesthetic featuring elements of paper, stone, and wood, the hotel boasts an expansive spa featuring an onsen-style bath and a pool, as well as distinguished dining establishments offering French and Italian culinary experiences.

Zentis, Osaka

Seek solace from Osaka's ceaseless energy in the welcoming embrace of Zentis in Dojimahama, where impeccable hotel design leaves a lasting impression. Spanning 16 floors, the soundproofed rooms exude airy tranquility, with many offering splendid city vistas. With a garden and terrace, this is an unparalleled oasis for respite, providing a sanctuary away from the vibrant and bustling ambiance of one of Japan's largest cities.

With the Style Fukuoka

This distinctive boutique hotel with 16 rooms is located in the cosmopolitan city of Fukuoka in western Japan. Designed to cater to those seeking a vibrant and energetic atmosphere, rather than tranquil surroundings, this establishment offers a cozy yet sophisticated experience. Guests can enjoy amenities such as a rooftop spa Jacuzzi, a pool, in-room spa treatments and massages, Italian and Teppanyaki Japanese restaurants, a water terrace, and colorful, spacious rooms. Attention to detail is evident throughout your stay, including the provision of a Japanese/Western breakfast, a minibar, and complimentary bicycle use.

Wise Owls Hostels Shibuya, Tokyo

The Shibuya neighborhood, known for its lively and neon-lit ambiance, is not typically associated with budget-friendly accommodations. Therefore, the presence of this hostel, offering private rooms, a female-only room with bunk beds, and mixed capsule-style dormitories, is particularly welcomed. The hostel provides a simple and functional environment, complete with communal kitchens, laundry facilities, and bathrooms. It also features a value-driven organic restaurant and convenient vending machines. Additionally, its location near the creative Nakameguro quarter allows for enjoyable experiences in fashion boutiques, cafes, and design studios situated along the canal.

Benesse House, Naoshima Island

Situated in Kagawa Prefecture, away from bustling cities and tourist destinations, Benesse House offers a unique concept as it combines a hotel with an extensive art museum showcasing paintings, sculptures, photography, and installations. The property, designed by renowned architect Tadao Ando, embraces a minimalist aesthetic using materials such as concrete, wood, and glass. While the bedrooms may be relatively small and simple, they offer delightful sea views and feature original artwork. The public areas, grounds, and surroundings also showcase art. The hotel's restaurant continues the minimalist theme and presents a menu inspired by French cuisine. However, it's important to note that the accommodation and dining costs are not minimal

Sowaka, Kyoto

Nestled on a tranquil side street in Higashiyama, Sowaka seamlessly blends the serene and traditional comforts of an old-style ryokan with the sophisticated elements of a modern boutique hotel. Located just steps away from the historic geisha district of Gion, Sowaka boasts a stunning Japanese-style garden and La Bombance Gion, an on-site restaurant led by a Michelin-starred team from the renowned La Bombance establishment in Tokyo.

The Shinmonzen, Tokyo

Designed by the esteemed architect Tadao Ando, The Shinmonzen exemplifies meticulous attention to detail in every aspect of its design. The nine suites within the hotel exhibit various themes, from those directly inspired by traditional ryokans with tatami floors, to others adorned with bamboo and stone accents. Each room offers a serene and visually pleasing ambiance, complemented by balcony views overlooking a similarly tranquil river.

St. Regis Osaka

Situated in the sophisticated Midosuji district, often referred to as the "Champs Elysées of Osaka," the St. Regis Osaka provides a stylish and comfortable retreat. The hotel's prime location offers easy access to shopping areas, the train station, the trendy Shinsaibashi district, and the vibrant Namba nightlife neighborhood. Guests can indulge in the Zen rooftop champagne garden, dine at the elegant Italian restaurant or French-style cafe, and unwind at the sophisticated bar, spa, and gym facilities. The luxurious rooms feature neutral decor, Nespresso machines, and splendid city views, making it an exceptional choice for a stay in Osaka. Don't miss the signature Shogun Mary cocktail, the Osaka adaptation of the original Bloody Mary created in 1934 at the inaugural St. Regis Hotel in New York.

Treeful Treehouse, Okinawa

Even without prior knowledge of Treeful Treehouse's commendable commitment to sustainability, one cannot deny its remarkable appeal as a truly spectacular accommodation. Nestled amidst the lush Okinawan jungle, Treeful Treehouse seamlessly combines eco-friendliness with an abundance of cozy luxury. Employing composting toilets and utilizing water from a well, every aspect of Treeful's design aims to minimize its impact on the surrounding habitat. The establishment proudly asserts its carbon-negative status, actively absorbing more carbon dioxide than it produces.

SHOPPING IN JAPAN

Japan stands as a veritable shopping paradise, offering a plethora of stores catering to diverse needs, ranging from traditional souvenirs and local delicacies to cutting-edge electronics and coveted fashion brands. Both domestic and international labels find representation, while shopping options cater to a range of budgets, from 100-yen shops to upscale fashion boutiques and department stores.

Major cities, such as Tokyo and Osaka, boast numerous shopping districts, each exuding its distinctive character and typically centered around major train stations. Shopping centers, covered arcades, and expansive underground malls also house an array of shops. Beyond city centers, prominent big box retailers, outlet malls, and suburban shopping centers present a wealth of choices, ensuring ample variety for shoppers.

Georgia Tucker

SHOPPING BASICS

HOW TO SHOP

Osaka's Tenjinbashi-Suji Shopping Arcade
Shopping in Japan is generally an enjoyable experience, characterized by polite, friendly, and attentive sales staff who prioritize providing exceptional customer service. While foreign language services are not commonly available, certain stores that frequently serve international customers may have staff members proficient in English or other languages.

Shopping Hours And Closures
Typically, larger shops and department stores operate daily from 10:00 to 20:00. Smaller establishments near tourist attractions may have shorter operating hours. Most stores remain open on weekends and national holidays, except January 1, when many establishments close. Large chain stores maintain daily operations, but smaller independent shops may observe a weekly or monthly closure.

Greeting
Upon entering a store, customers are warmly greeted by the sales staff with the expression "irasshaimase," meaning "welcome, please come in." While it is not expected for customers to respond verbally, this courteous gesture sets the tone for a pleasant shopping experience.

Georgia Tucker

A SEAWEED SHOP IN THE BASEMENT OF A DEPARTMENT STORE

CONSUMPTION TAX AND TAX-FREE SHOPPING
In Japan, the consumption tax, equivalent to VAT, GST, or sales tax in other countries, is a flat rate of 10 percent on most items, excluding food, drinks, and newspaper subscriptions, which are taxed at 8 percent (excluding alcoholic beverages and dining out). Retailers are required to display price tags that include the tax, although some may also indicate pre-tax prices alongside the total amount, resulting in price tags showing two prices.

Foreign tourists have the option of tax-free shopping at authorized stores when making purchases exceeding 5000 yen in a single store or shopping complex on a given calendar day. A valid passport is necessary for tax-free shopping. It is important to note that in many stores, customers are required to initially pay the full price, including the consumption tax, at the cashier and then obtain a refund at a designated customer service desk.

Please be aware that goods purchased in Japan may be subject to import duties upon arrival in your home country. Additionally, it is important to consider differences in operating voltages, language settings, and other standards that may apply to products bought in Japan.

PAYMENT
Cash is widely accepted throughout Japan, and it is generally acceptable to use large bills for small purchases, except at smaller

street vendors or local shops. Japanese yen can be withdrawn from ATMs using foreign bank accounts.

Credit cards, while not universally accepted as cash, can be used in most stores, particularly major retail establishments, electronics shops, and department stores. Visa, Mastercard, JCB, American Express, and Union Pay are among the most widely accepted credit card types.

The use of IC cards, such as Suica, and other mobile payment methods is increasingly becoming available for purchases at various shops and restaurants across Japan. Cash, credit cards, and IC cards

SHOPPING MANNERS

When making a payment, it is customary to place the money on the provided tray, preferably with bills neatly unfolded. Change may also be returned in the same manner.

Bargaining is generally not a common practice and is not appreciated in most stores.

WRAPPING

Once a purchase has been made, items are typically placed in bags or marked with colored tape. Some stores may charge a nominal fee for bags. Clothing stores, department stores, and gift shops often offer complimentary gift wrapping services upon request, although some stores may apply a minimal fee for this service.

TYPES OF STORES

Japan offers a diverse range of shops and shopping areas. The following are common types that travelers are likely to encounter:

Department Stores

Department stores are found in major cities across Japan and are renowned for offering high-quality products and exceptional customer service. Consequently, prices at department stores tend to be higher. The basement food sections of department stores are particularly noteworthy and can be considered tourist attractions, while the restaurant floors offer a convenient selection of moderately priced dining options.

Electronics Stores

Electronics chains such as Yodobashi Camera, Bic Camera, and Yamada Denki carry a wide range of electronic goods, including computers, cameras, cell phones, home appliances, toys, movies, games, gadgets, and accessories. Many of these chains operate large-scale stores near major train stations. Notable areas known for their electronic stores include Tokyo's Akihabara, Shinjuku, and Ikebukuro districts, as well as Osaka's Den Den Town.

100 Yen Shops

100 yen shops offer a diverse array of products, each priced at 100 yen (plus consumption tax), making them popular destinations for budget-conscious travelers and residents. Several chains operate 100 yen stores throughout Japan.

Convenience Stores
With over 40,000 locations spread across the country, convenience stores, known as Konbini, are open 24/7 and provide a wide range of food, beverages, essential household items, and various services, including ATMs, shipping, and ticketing services. Convenience stores truly live up to their name, offering unparalleled convenience to customers.

Shopping Malls
Shopping malls can be found in both urban centers and rural areas. These establishments are typically dominated by clothing stores and often include designated floors or food courts for dining, as well as movie theaters and videogame arcades.

Shopping Arcades
Shopping arcades, present in nearly all medium to large cities, are characterized by nostalgic, older shopping streets comprised of numerous stores and restaurants. Many of these arcades are covered, providing shelter from the elements. Noteworthy examples include the extended arcades in Osaka, Sendai, and Takamatsu.

Underground Malls
In major cities where space is at a premium, underground malls are commonly situated around or beneath significant railway stations. In some instances, multiple underground malls interconnect, forming extensive subterranean networks. Tokyo

and Osaka boast some of the most expansive underground malls, reflecting their urban prominence.

Temple And Shrine Approaches
The paths leading to popular temples and shrines are traditionally lined with shops and restaurants catering to pilgrims and tourists. Particularly vibrant examples include Nakamise, situated near Tokyo's Sensoji Temple, and the approach to Kiyomizudera Temple in Kyoto.

Public Markets
Public markets teem with vendors and restaurants offering an array of fresh fish, vegetables, meat, and prepared foods. Often serving both the culinary industry and the general public, these markets tend to operate with earlier opening and closing hours compared to other shopping districts. Exploring the gastronomic side of Japan provides an enjoyable experience. Renowned markets include Tokyo's Tsukiji Outer Market, Kyoto's Nishiki Market, Kanazawa's Omicho Market, and Hakodate's Morning Market.

Supermarkets
Supermarkets in Japan follow a similar organizational structure to their counterparts worldwide. They are most prevalent in suburban areas and medium-sized cities and towns. However, locating supermarkets within the heart of Japan's largest cities can be more challenging.

Flea Markets

For enthusiasts of flea markets, Japan offers excellent venues showcasing a diverse range of new and used art, crafts, clothing, traditional goods, antiques, food, jewelry, tools, and weapons. Notable flea markets are held at Kyoto's Toji Temple and Kitano Tenmangu Shrine.

Outlet Malls

Usually situated on the outskirts of major cities, near airports, or along expressways, outlet malls attract those seeking discounted brand-name goods. While prices may be more favorable compared to regular retail shops, it is important to note that the level of discounts and bargains might not be as substantial as anticipated at an outlet establishment. Nevertheless, outlet malls provide an enjoyable shopping experience for enthusiasts. Among the largest and most popular is the Gotemba Premium Outlets.

Georgia Tucker

Georgia Tucker

CHAPTER NINE

LANGUAGE AND COMMUNICATION IN JAPAN

JAPANESE BODY LANGUAGE: A GUIDE TO NONVERBAL COMMUNICATION IN JAPAN

Japan is renowned for its illustrious heritage, steeped in traditional customs and a flourishing culture. A fundamental element of this culture, essential for visitors to comprehend, is the distinctive realm of Japanese body language. Proficiency in understanding these nonverbal cues can significantly enhance communication and foster meaningful interactions with Japanese individuals. Presented below are several common gestures of body language in Japan, along with their respective meanings:

Bowing Culture
Bowing holds deep-rooted significance in Japanese tradition, serving as a reverential gesture. It serves multiple purposes, such as expressing greetings, demonstrating gratitude or apology, and displaying respect towards elders or those in superior positions. The depth of a bow is contingent upon the specific context and the relationship between the individuals involved. Let us explore the various types of bows together.

A Lady Bowing

• A shallow bow is commonly employed in informal or casual settings. It entails an inclination of approximately 15 degrees, which is considered the standard or casual norm, as exemplified in the illustration below:

• A deeper bow is reserved for formal or respectful salutations, typically requiring an inclination of 30 degrees or more. It is crucial to bear in mind that such a bow is regarded as an exceedingly respectful gesture, as depicted below:

Bowing also adheres to specific protocols and etiquette. For instance, it is customary for an individual of lower status to initiate the bow, while the person of higher standing should bow last. It is essential to recognize that bowing is deeply embedded within the cultural fabric of Japan, and not everyone in the country may engage in this practice when interacting with foreigners. Hence, it is advisable to observe and emulate the conduct of the Japanese individuals with whom you engage.

Eye Contact Customs

In Japan, avoiding direct eye contact is considered an act of respect and humility. Prolonged eye contact, particularly while conversing with elders or individuals in positions of authority, is deemed impolite. Specifically, maintaining eye contact is regarded as confrontational and assertive, qualities that do not always align with the values of harmony, collectivism, and politeness revered in Japanese culture. Instead, a sign of humility and respect is to avert one's gaze slightly downward or away from the person's eyes. It is worth noting that this stands in contrast to the teachings of many Western cultures, where sustained eye contact is viewed as a sign of honesty and engagement, while a lack of eye contact may be interpreted as dishonesty or disinterest.

Eye Contact

Hand Gestures
- **Indicate A Direction:** Pointing with one's finger is considered impolite in Japan. Instead, employing an open hand gesture or using the entire hand to indicate the direction is more appropriate. For instance, when indicating a location or a specific object, it is customary to employ an open-hand gesture in the general direction rather than pointing with the index finger.

- **Gift Exchange:** During the act of giving or receiving an item, it is considered respectful to employ both hands. This gesture signifies humility, and respect, and conveys a sense of treating the object with care.

- **Touch Someone Without Permission:** Touching another person's body or possessions without permission is deemed impolite. This includes refraining from touching someone's face or interfering with their kimono or yukata attire without prior consent.

- **Counting With Fingers:** The manner of counting with fingers in Japan differs from many Western cultures. Traditional Japanese counting, known as "Soroban" counting, involves employing an abacus—a frame adorned with beads used for counting. While counting with fingers is also practiced, it diverges from the Western approach. Japanese individuals begin with an open hand, commencing from the thumb and gradually closing it as they proceed.

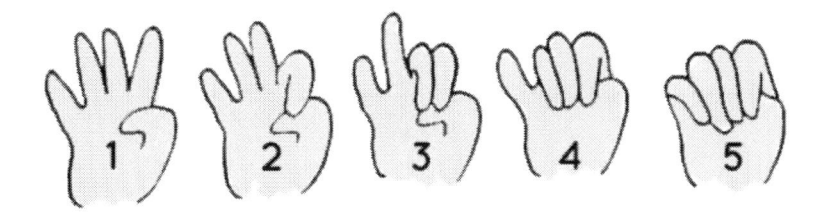

•**Talking About Oneself:** When discussing oneself, a common gesture among Japanese individuals involves pointing the index finger upward toward their face. This gesture signifies that one is referring to themselves, as depicted in the accompanying illustration.

•**Asking For the Bill:** To request the check at a restaurant, Japanese individuals often form an X shape with their hands, as shown below.

Asking For Bill

•**Saying OK**: Agreeing with something can be conveyed by forming a circle with the thumb and index finger, symbolizing "O.K," as illustrated:

•**Saying No**: Although rare to witness, Japanese individuals may employ a specific hand gesture to politely decline a compliment or express a general "no." This gesture involves waving one hand in front of the lower face.

By gaining insight into these nonverbal cues, one can navigate communication more effectively in Japan and demonstrate respect for its culture. It is important to remember that body language can vary depending on the context, so attentive observation and respectful conduct are always advisable when uncertainty arises.

JAPANESE CULTURE AND TRADITION

An Extensive Exploration of the Enigmatic Land of the Rising Sun

Japan boasts a vibrant culture with a rich historical tapestry spanning thousands of years, tracing its roots back to prehistoric times as early as 14,500 BC. Showcasing an exquisite fusion of elegance, simplicity, and formality, Japan stands as a bastion of extraordinary cultural offerings admired worldwide. However, certain aspects of Japanese culture may appear unfamiliar and inaccessible to individuals from Western backgrounds. Rest assured, as we embark on an immersive crash course that unveils the myriad facets of Japan, encompassing its language, cuisine, and the captivating realm of anime. Prepare to delve into the depths of this captivating realm!

The History And Influences Of Japanese Culture

Ancient Japan experienced significant influences from China and Korea, shaping various aspects of its culture. Technological advancements such as rice farming and ironwork were introduced from these neighboring countries. Buddhism found its way into Japan through the Korean peninsula, while the adoption of Chinese characters gave rise to Japanese kanji.

Even the beloved tradition of tea drinking was initially imported from China, brought back to Japan by Buddhist monks who had studied in China during the 8th century.

The teachings of Confucianism, also originating from the Asian mainland, permeated throughout Japan, leading to the development of a collective-oriented culture. According to Confucian principles, the harmony of the group takes precedence over individual emotions. Consequently, the Japanese people perceive themselves as part of a collective whole, making conscientious efforts to act in the best interests of those around them, thus upholding integrity. The ability to read the atmosphere, known as "kūki o yomu" (空気を読む), is essential in all situations, ensuring that everyone's sentiments are considered before individual decisions are made.

However, it is important to note that Japan also boasts its indigenous customs and traditions.

Japanese customs revolve around the four distinct seasons, a significant focus in the country. Each season—warm and pleasant spring, hot and humid summer, crisp and blustery autumn, and cool and frosty winter—holds great significance in Japanese life. Seasonal activities such as cherry blossom viewing (hanami) in spring and wearing yukata (a casual version of the kimono) during summer festivals are eagerly anticipated. Moreover, different types of cuisine are enjoyed based on the time of year.

Another notable aspect of Japanese culture is the immense influence of Tokyo. Beginning in feudal times, when nobility and military officials were required to reside in Tokyo, a unified "Tokyo culture" emerged as the prevailing standard throughout Japan. With a quarter of Japan's population residing in the Tokyo Metropolitan Area, Tokyo serves as the nation's political, financial, and cultural hub. It often finds itself at the center of attention, not unlike how New York or Los Angeles represent cultural touchstones in the United States—albeit occasionally being attacked by giant monsters in movies!

THE LANGUAGE OF JAPAN

Japanese, spoken by 125 million people worldwide, is renowned for its complexity. With three writing systems, intricate grammatical structures, and a hierarchical language style, mastering Japanese can be a challenge. However, let's begin with an introduction.

Japanese is considered a language isolate, unrelated to any other known language. This unique status gives the Japanese its distinct structure, setting it apart from all other languages in the world.

Japanese Pronunciation

Despite the overall complexity of Japanese, pronunciation is relatively straightforward. Spoken Japanese consists of 15 consonants and only five vowels, making it relatively easy to pronounce once the accent is grasped. These consonants and vowels combine to form syllables, which are conveyed using hiragana and katakana. Interestingly, every syllable is pronounced uniformly, regardless of its position within a sentence. In this aspect, English could learn a few things from Japanese!

Japanese Writing

Speaking of writing systems, hiragana, and katakana are two indigenous scripts used in Japanese writing. They are categorized as syllabaries, wherein each character represents a single syllable (consonant + vowel) in the language. On the other hand, kanji was borrowed from China and functions as a pictographic system, with each character representing an idea. It's worth noting that hiragana and katakana were derived from kanji.

Japanese Speech

Japanese exhibit gendered speech, featuring distinct speech styles for men and women. The primary differences can be observed in personal pronouns and sentence-ending particles.

In Japanese, various pronouns are used to refer to oneself. For instance, "あたし" is exclusively used by females, while "俺 (おれ)" is exclusively used by males. "私 (わたし)" can be used by individuals of any gender.

Regarding sentence-ending particles, which are grammatical elements that enhance the meaning of a sentence, certain particles are more commonly associated with a specific gender. "わ," "なの," and "かしら" are preferred by women, whereas "ぞ," "ぜ," and "よ" are used in rougher, male speech.

Furthermore, Japan boasts diverse regional dialects throughout the country. From Hokkaido to Osaka, and down to Okinawa, various forms of the Japanese language exist, creating unique linguistic differences. The way a person speaks in Fukuoka may sound markedly distinct to someone from Aomori.

JAPANESE RELIGION AND SPIRITUALITY
An Exploration of Cultural Beliefs and Customs

Japan encompasses a harmonious coexistence of two major religions: Shinto and Buddhism. These religious traditions permeate everyday life, with influences from both Shinto and Buddhism evident in various aspects of Japanese society. Shinto shrines can be found within Buddhist temple premises, and it is common for individuals in Japan to partake in Shinto weddings and   Buddhist   funerals.

Shintoism

Shinto, the indigenous religion of Japan, centers around the veneration of kami (神, かみ) — divine beings that are believed to inhabit all facets of existence, including animals and natural elements such as mountains. While the terms "god" or "spirit" are often used to describe kami, they fail to fully capture the profound essence of these natural forces. Kami evokes a sense of awe and reverence, manifesting in various forms, places, objects, and even individuals.

Shrines are constructed as sanctuaries dedicated to housing and worshiping kami. It is within these sacred spaces that rituals of worship and offerings are performed to honor these deities. The responsibility of conducting these rituals and tending to the shrines traditionally falls upon priests and shrine maidens known as miko (巫女, みこ). Shinto, unlike an organized religion with rigid doctrines and holy texts, is characterized more by a collection of customs and traditions.

Buddhism

Buddhism was introduced to Japan through the Korean kingdom of Baekje. In essence, Buddhism encompasses diverse spiritual paths that seek to liberate individuals from earthly suffering and the cycle of rebirth by attaining enlightenment.

Initially embraced by the ruling class of Japan, Buddhism eventually gained acceptance among the general populace. Its teachings spread throughout the country, resulting in the construction of grand temples and the travel of monks to China for study.

Over time, Buddhism in Japan developed into various sects, including Nichiren, Pure Land, and Zen Buddhism. Each sect possesses distinct practices, yet they all emphasize the cultivation of a pure heart and mind through diligent engagement in rituals and introspective meditation.

Other Religions

While religions such as Christianity and Islam are not widely prevalent in Japan, the country does observe certain aspects of these religions. For instance, Christmas is celebrated in Japan as a romantic holiday.

It is worth noting, however, that Japan's religious practices are not overtly devout among the general populace. Rather, religious rituals are often observed as cultural traditions or habits. Visiting shrines and temples to seek blessings or good fortune is commonplace, and numerous festivals take place at Shinto shrines. During New Year's, people flock to shrines for their first visit of the year, while Buddhist temples ring bells 108 times to dispel misfortune from the previous year.

Superstition And Japan

Superstition holds a significant place in Japanese culture, surpassing the boundaries of organized religion. Many superstitions stem from ancient folklore and involve word associations, as the Japanese language contains numerous homophones — words pronounced the same but with different meanings.

For instance, "yakudoshi" (厄年, やくどし) refers to unlucky years in an individual's life when they are believed to be more susceptible to misfortune. Certain numbers, such as 4 and 9, symbolize death and suffering, respectively, and are thus avoided in room numbers and gift-giving.

Fortune-telling is also popular, with many individuals visiting shrines to receive fortunes or make wishes to the gods.

JAPANESE CUSTOMS AND TRADITIONS

Japan, as a society, upholds numerous unique customs rooted in traditions that have endured for millennia. These customs are regarded as integral components of Japanese identity.

Georgia Tucker

Here are some noteworthy aspects of modern-day Japan, providing a glimpse into the current cultural landscape:

• Clothing reflects a tendency towards modesty, with muted colors and concealing attire compared to Western fashion. While colorful Lolita dresses may not be the norm, traditional clothing is still worn during festivals and significant ceremonies.

• Tattoos carry traditional associations with the yakuza, the Japanese mafia, who often adorn themselves with elaborate full-body tattoos denoting their affiliations. Consequently, visible tattoos may elicit curiosity or surprise. However, younger generations in Japan may display more acceptance towards tattoos.

• The beginning of a romantic relationship in Japan is often marked by a mutual confession of feelings. Affection is typically expressed through subtle gestures rather than overt displays of physical intimacy. Public displays of kissing, for instance, are generally considered inappropriate.

- Mascots play a multifaceted role beyond their endearing appearances. Japan's mascots are renowned for their cuteness and serve as representative symbols for companies, products, cities, and various causes. These beloved characters contribute to promoting tourism and raising awareness of significant issues.

Japan's profound blend of religious practices, superstitions, and cherished customs shape a society that values its cultural heritage. By appreciating and understanding these customs, one gains a deeper insight into the fabric of Japanese life.

Manners And Etiquette In Japan

Japan is renowned for its culture of respect and adherence to etiquette. Whether it involves removing your shoes before entering someone's home or offering your seat to an elderly person on a train, displaying good manners is essential for harmonious interactions in Japan.

- Through gestures and actions, the Japanese people nurture their relationships and prioritize group harmony. Here are some fundamental guidelines to bear in mind:

- When entering someone's house, it is crucial to remove your shoes—a practice that cannot be emphasized enough.

- Maintain silence and ensure your phone is on silent mode when using public transportation.
- Avoid sticking your chopsticks upright in a bowl of rice, as this is customary only during funerals. Refrain from playing with your chopsticks as well.
- Carry your garbage with you until you locate an appropriate bin for disposal.
- Stand on the designated side of the escalator to facilitate smooth flow and movement.

Japanese Formality

Japanese society is deeply rooted in formality and hierarchy. When interacting with others, Japanese individuals consider factors such as age, occupation, social status, and familiarity to determine their choice of words and actions.

Japanese formality is characterized by a set of intricate rules and customs that may initially appear overwhelming. However, there is no expectation for you to master them all. For those interested in navigating the realm of Japanese formality, here are a few insights to assist you in engaging with polite Japanese society:

Formal Japanese encompasses distinct levels of speech, ranging from casual to polite language known as Keigo. These levels enable you to demonstrate the appropriate level of respect for your conversation partner.

Seiza is the formal way of sitting, particularly during formal occasions like elaborate dinners. It involves sitting on the floor with legs tucked underneath and hands placed on thighs (for men) or folded in the lap (for women).

Bowing holds great significance in Japanese culture, symbolizing respect. However, different situations warrant varying degrees of bowing. A casual bow, known as shaku, is at a 15° angle, while Keira is performed at 30°-45° for bosses or in-laws, with a deeper bow indicating greater respect. Visiting temples or making profound apologies calls for a deep and prolonged bow of 70°.

JAPANESE WORK AND BUSINESS CULTURE

The Japanese business world is known for its strict formalities and rigid structure. Specific protocols govern seating arrangements, greetings with superiors and clients, as well as displaying due deference.

If you intend to engage in business with Japanese companies, it is advisable to familiarize yourself with the disparities between your own country's work culture and that of Japan.

Business Cards

The practice of exchanging business cards, known as (名刺交換, めいしこうかん) in Japanese, is a customary and essential aspect of establishing meaningful connections with Japanese contacts. Business cards are regarded as a representation of an individual's identity and must be treated with utmost respect.

Workplace Hierarchy

Respect and adherence to strict hierarchies are fundamental in the Japanese workplace. Seniority holds significant importance, with longer-tenured employees enjoying higher wages and better promotional opportunities. Due to the emphasis on hierarchy, Japanese employees are expected to consult their supervisors regarding any issues or decisions. In Japan, an employee who diligently seeks guidance from their superiors before making choices is considered commendable, in contrast to the independent and proactive approach valued in Western cultures.

Socialization After Work

Japanese businessmen understand the value of relaxation and camaraderie. Engaging in social activities such as gathering at bars or karaoke establishments with colleagues, a practice known as "nomikai," (飲み会, のみかい), is commonplace and serves to foster stronger relationships within the team. These informal social settings provide an opportunity for coworkers to express their grievances and frustrations related to work, as the strict social regulations of the workplace are more relaxed. On occasion, a smaller group may venture for a "nijikai," (二次会にじかい)or "second party," where the atmosphere can become livelier and more festive.

FOOD AND DRINK IN JAPANESE CULTURE

The thought of Japanese cuisine, with its mouthwatering sushi, ramen, and tempura, evokes great anticipation. However, Japanese culinary culture extends far beyond what is commonly found in local teriyaki establishments.

Georgia Tucker

Traditional Japanese cuisine, known as "washoku," (和食, わしょく, Japanese food) is celebrated for its simplicity, clean flavors, and regional variations. Food holds significant importance in Japanese culture, with an emphasis on achieving a harmonious balance of colors, flavors, and nutritional elements in each meal. Fish and seafood serve as staple sources of protein, while a diverse range of delectable meat dishes, such as yakitori, also contribute to the culinary repertoire. Miso soup and pickled vegetables are ubiquitous features of washoku menus, complemented by the delightful presence of fluffy white rice.

When it comes to beverages, tea holds a cherished place in Japanese culture. The country boasts an abundance of tea varieties, with warm and cold options readily available in vending machines nationwide. Green tea, oolong tea, and black tea, among others, exhibit the diversity and richness of the Japanese tea tradition, which merits extensive exploration.

Alcohol also plays a notable role in Japanese social customs. From traditional sake to chūhai and beer, the Japanese people appreciate their libations, and many bonding experiences among colleagues take place over glasses of beer at izakayas. During these social gatherings, it is customary to prioritize filling the glasses of friends before one's own, preferably before they become empty, demonstrating an expression of consideration and camaraderie.

JAPANESE SPORTS CULTURE
A Celebration of Physical Activities and Traditional Competitions

Japan embraces a vibrant sports culture, encompassing a diverse array of athletic pursuits ranging from martial arts to modern sports. Notably, the nation commemorates this enthusiasm through the observance of "Health and Sports Day," a dedicated holiday that unites schools and communities in large-scale athletic events.

Baseball occupies a position of prominence as Japan's most popular sport, captivating thousands of spectators annually with events like the Japan Series and High School Baseball Championships. Certain Japanese players have attained celebrity status beyond Japan's borders, with Ichiro Suzuki of the Seattle Mariners being widely recognized as one of the most illustrious ballplayers of all time.

Tennis, soccer, and golf also enjoy popularity throughout the country, serving as both recreational pastimes and avenues for competitive engagement. However, traditional Japanese sports retain their appeal as well. Sumo, originating as a Shinto ritual, has evolved into a captivating wrestling match where colossal athletes strive to force each other out of the ring, earning it the unofficial distinction of being Japan's national sport.

Japanese Martial Arts
Japanese martial arts provide a glimpse into Japan's rich cultural heritage. Judo, a martial art emphasizing technical takedowns of opponents, has achieved global recognition and even garnered its Olympic category. Kendo, rooted in samurai techniques, showcases dueling practitioners engaging in spirited bouts with bamboo blades, accompanied by spirited shouts. Additionally, Japanese archery, known as kyudo, employs large, potent bows, with a dedicated subset focusing on horseback shooting. The realm of Japanese sports is truly boundless, encompassing diverse disciplines such as aikido and jujitsu.

JAPANESE ART CULTURE
Japanese art's allure has captivated generations, embodying aesthetics characterized by elegance and simplicity. Some art forms have been meticulously honed over centuries, while others have emerged more recently. Regardless of their medium, all forms of Japanese art share a distinctive essence.

Japanese Anime
No discussion of Japanese art would be complete without mentioning anime. This animated medium has garnered global popularity and serves as a prominent gateway to Japan's artistic culture. Countless classics, including "Astro Boy," "Dragon Ball," and "Naruto," have achieved household recognition. Interestingly, anime traces its origins back to the Edo period when a form of entertainment known as utsushi-e gained popularity among the masses. This form involved projecting glass

slides through a wooden lantern. Presently, Japan boasts over 400 animation companies that have produced a vast array of shows and movies.

Japanese Authors
Murasaki Shikibu, the author of "The Tale of Genji," considered Japan her home. Japan's literary tradition remains rich and thriving, owing to the contributions of Japanese authors across the centuries. Many of these writers have achieved worldwide acclaim, including figures such as Kenzaburo Oe and Haruki Murakami. Short stories occupy a significant place in Japanese literature, with collections published in books and monthly magazines. It is no wonder that reading enjoys widespread popularity in Japan.

Japanese Entertainment
Japan boasts an array of media icons, including renowned figures like Akira Kurosawa, Utada Hikaru, and Takuya Kimura. Noteworthy Japanese films such as "Godzilla" and "The Ring" have captivated audiences globally, reflecting historical and thematic elements prevalent in Japan. Moreover, Japanese singers have crafted music that resonates with the general populace and niche communities alike.

Gaining a deeper understanding of Japanese culture can be facilitated through the exploration of Japanese movies and music, particularly when utilizing language learning programs like FluentU, which employ authentic content. FluentU's interactive subtitles provide learners with opportunities to grasp the nuances of the Japanese language as native speakers employ it, both on web platforms and mobile devices (iOS and Android).

Japanese Theater

Traditional Japanese theater holds an indelible place in the country's cultural fabric. Kabuki theater, renowned for its thrilling and stylistic performances, features actors donning vibrant masks. In contrast, Noh theater showcases refined movements and meticulously crafted poetic narratives, rooted in performances at religious ceremonies. Bunraku, a form of puppet theater masterfully manipulated by skilled performers, continues to captivate audiences in the 21st century, much as it did during the 16th century in Edo.

Japanese Traditional Arts

One of the prominent aspects of Japan's rich cultural heritage lies in its traditional arts, with the tea ceremony being a remarkable example. The tea ceremony is a meticulously performed ritual that involves the preparation of matcha tea accompanied by delightful confections, symbolizing the epitome of hospitality. This highly formal ceremony encompasses the use of bamboo utensils to serve and whisk the tea, following a precise sequence of steps, all aimed at offering guests a cup of dense green tea.

In addition to the tea ceremony, other traditional arts hold significance in Japanese culture. Calligraphy, for instance, transforms the act of writing Japanese kanji into an elegant and flowing form of artistic expression. Ikebana, the art of arranging flowers in a specific aesthetic style, is another notable art form in Japan.

Various institutions, such as schools, universities, and community centers, provide opportunities for individuals to engage in these arts. Clubs dedicated to practicing these traditions can be found in educational institutions, while community centers organize classes and events that welcome participation from both locals and tourists.

With its diverse array of cultural offerings, Japan captivates individuals with different interests, be it sports, arts, cuisine, or beyond. Exploring the customs and history of Japan not only unveils the mysteries of this Asian nation but also humanizes its people. It is possible that embarking on such a journey may ignite a lifelong fascination with all things Japanese.

Georgia Tucker

LANGUAGE BARRIERS IN JAPAN? TRAVEL IN JAPAN WITHOUT SPEAKING JAPANESE

OVERCOMING LANGUAGE BARRIERS IN JAPAN.

First-time travelers to Japan may initially feel apprehensive about potential language barriers during their visit. However, there is no need to worry, as Japan continues to enhance its tourist-friendly environment. The following tips offer guidance on how to travel in Japan without speaking Japanese:

Tips For Overcoming Language Barriers: How To Travel In Japan Without Speaking Japanese

Observe the behavior of locals and learn from their social etiquette. Take note of their politeness and quiet demeanor while using public transportation, avoiding distractions from mobile devices.

Japanese people are generally friendly and helpful, particularly when approached with politeness. However, it is important to acknowledge that unfriendly individuals exist in every society.

Be mindful of proper manners and etiquette.

Acquire a pre-paid data SIM card to access Google Maps for directions and utilize Google Translate for communication with locals.

Engaging in casual conversations with random strangers may be less common among locals, who often prefer to keep to themselves. If seeking interactions, it is more likely to occur with fellow foreign travelers.

Speaking louder does not facilitate communication. Japanese culture values politeness, so approaching others with respect and speaking considerately is key.

Georgia Tucker

USEFUL JAPANESE EXPRESSIONS WHILE TRAVELING IN JAPAN

MORE USEFUL JAPANESE EXPRESSIONS

Tips For Restaurants

Inquire about the availability of an English menu from the host or staff.

Before entering a restaurant, examine the plastic food display, which showcases the dishes with remarkable accuracy, providing a visual guide to the menu.

Use hand gestures to indicate the number of items you wish to order.

In many restaurants, you may receive your bill while still eating. This signals that payment should be made at the counter near the restaurant's entrance, streamlining the turnover process and allowing for efficient table cleaning for subsequent guests.

Tips For Visiting Major Attractions

It is highly recommended to acquire a pre-paid data SIM card or a mobile WiFi device to ensure seamless navigation while exploring Japan's major attractions. Google Maps, offering comprehensive train and subway instructions, makes this a necessity. For a detailed comparison of SIM card companies in Japan, refer to the provided resource.

When utilizing train and subway stations, locate the yellow information maps, which provide valuable guidance on selecting the appropriate exit leading to your desired destination. These maps are available in English.

Along the way to popular tourist sites, signage will be strategically placed to assist you in reaching your destination.

Tips For Using Public Transportation

English signs are prominently displayed in transportation hubs across major cities, facilitating smooth navigation to your intended destinations.

Should you require assistance, locate the information counters or kiosks where station employees are available to provide guidance.

Communication with taxi drivers can present challenges. In such instances, consult with the concierge or bell station at your hotel to obtain a taxi card. This card will feature the Japanese characters corresponding to your destination, allowing you to easily communicate with the driver upon returning to your hotel.

Alternatively, consider utilizing Uber, available exclusively in Tokyo. This platform ensures clear communication by inputting your destination into the GPS, and many Uber drivers in Tokyo are proficient in English.

Japan places great emphasis on facilitating communication with international travelers. As a result, an increasing number of illustrations can be found at stations and on trains/subways, guiding tourists on appropriate behavior following Japanese culture and norms.

HACKS TO WORK AROUND THE LANGUAGE BARRIER IN JAPAN

Japan stands as one of the world's most enchanting destinations, attracting countless travelers. However, navigating the country can be challenging due to the language barrier. To overcome this obstacle, several language barrier hacks can be employed to enhance your experience in Japan. Before delving into these tips, it is crucial to prioritize obtaining a portable WiFi device or a SIM card with data connectivity. This will ensure access to the internet, offering invaluable assistance throughout your journey.

1. Download A Translation App, Or Have Google Translate Available
Having a translation app at your disposal, or access to Google Translate, can greatly aid in translating your inquiries from English to Japanese. This empowers you to confidently seek assistance from individuals you encounter, as people in Japan are generally eager to help.

2. Have Photos Ready for The Essentials
Prepare photos of essential locations such as restrooms, convenience stores like 7/11, train and bus stations, or specific tourist destinations you wish to visit. Displaying these images to locals will facilitate effective communication and prompt assistance when navigating through unfamiliar areas.

3. LEARN THESE SIMPLE JAPANESE PHRASES
ENGLISH TO JAPANESE (NIHONGO)

- Please- Onegaishimasu
- Thank you- Arigatou gozaimasu
- Excuse me- Sumimasen
- Yes - Hai
- No- Iie
- I'm Sorry- Gomen nasai
- I don't understand- Wakarimasen

Japanese people value politeness, and by utilizing these essential phrases, you can reciprocate their courtesy. Acquiring a basic understanding of these expressions will enhance your interactions and contribute to a more enjoyable experience during your trip.

In addition to these valuable language barrier hacks, exercise discretion when seeking assistance, particularly in bustling cities like Tokyo and Osaka. Be mindful of individuals who may be busy or in a hurry, selecting appropriate sources for inquiries to ensure minimal inconvenience to others.

Georgia Tucker

Georgia Tucker

CHAPTER TEN

THE TOP 10 TOURIST ATTRACTIONS IN JAPAN

Japan offers a wealth of captivating attractions, ranging from quaint villages and breathtaking Buddhist temples to open-air museums and awe-inspiring skyscrapers. Before your visit, familiarize yourself with the ten best tourist attractions that are simply unmissable!

Mount Fuji

As one of Japan's revered mountains, Mount Fuji stands proudly at an elevation of 3,776 meters. To behold the clearest vistas of Mount Fuji, plan your visit between December and January. Although the peak is often veiled by clouds, mornings typically afford a glimpse of its majesty. For the most remarkable views,

Georgia Tucker

consider visiting Koyo-Dai, Chureito Pagoda, Route 134, Mt. Fuji Panorama Ropeway, or Izunokuni Panorama Park.

Shirakawago Village

Located in Ōno District, Gifu Prefecture, Shirakawago Village has earned recognition as a UNESCO World Heritage Site. The village exudes charm, characterized by its traditional gassho-zukuri houses dating back to the 1800s. If you yearn for a day immersed in nature's embrace, this captivating locale is a highly recommended destination, nestled amidst rice paddies, mountains, and towering trees.

Location: Ōno District, Gifu Prefecture, Japan

Hiroshima Peace Memorial Park

The Hiroshima Peace Memorial Park, also known as Genbaku Dome, stands as the solitary surviving structure following the devastation caused by the atomic bomb in 1945. Once employed as an exhibition space for local products, the Genbaku Dome now resides within a park erected at the heart of Hiroshima to honor the victims of the nuclear attack. Entry to the park is free, and for deeper insights into this pivotal historical event, a visit to the adjacent Hiroshima Peace Memorial Museum is highly recommended.

Entry Fee (Museum): Adults ¥200, high school students ¥100, junior high school students and younger children enter free of charge, visitors aged 65 and above can enter for ¥100

Location: 1 丁目-1-10 Nakajimacho, Naka Ward, Hiroshima, 730-0811, Japan

Ōhori Park

Renowned for its captivating natural splendor, Ōhori Park showcases traditional Japanese gardens, a scenic trail encircling a serene lake, picturesque bridges, and an abundance of cherry blossom trees. This central Fukuoka gem is a perfect haven for leisurely walks and invigorating jogs.

Location: Chūō-ku, Fukuoka, Japan

Osaka Castle

Osaka Castle stands as one of Japan's most prominent and frequently visited attractions. Constructed by renowned Japanese warrior Toyotomi Hideyoshi in 1586, this castle played a pivotal role during the Azuchi-Momoyama period in Japan's unification. The castle's awe-inspiring architecture alone is a testament to its grandeur.

Georgia Tucker

Location: Japan, 〒540-0002 Osaka, Chuo Ward, Osakajo, 1番1号

Entry Fee (Castle & Museum): Adults and children aged 15 and above ¥600, children under 15 enter for free

Golden Pavilion

Kinkaku-Ji, widely known as the Golden Pavilion, is an iconic Buddhist temple in Kyoto. This resplendent structure features two levels adorned in gold leaf, combining elements of the Shinden and Bukke architectural styles. Please note that visitors are not permitted to enter the temple itself; however, you are welcome to explore the gardens, admire the temple from the outside, and enjoy the serene tea garden and gift shop.

Entry Fee (Garden Area): Adults ¥400, children ¥300

Location: 1 Kinkakujicho, Kita Ward, Kyoto, 603-8361, Japan

Tokyo Imperial Palace

The esteemed Tokyo Imperial Palace serves as the official residence of Japan's Imperial Family. Enclosed by sturdy stone walls, adorned with charming bridges, and encompassing a vast park, this architectural marvel offers a captivating experience. Generally, access to the inner grounds is limited, except on January 2 and February 23, when visitors can participate in the New Year's Greeting and Emperor's Birthday events. Enhance your visit by embarking on a guided tour around the park, providing insightful commentary for approximately an hour.

Location: 1-1 Chiyoda, Chiyoda City, Tokyo 100-8111, Japan

Itsukushima Shrine

Renowned as one of Japan's most beloved UNESCO World Heritage Sites, the Island Shrine of Itsukushima, located in Hatsukaichi, Hiroshima Prefecture, captivates visitors with its awe-inspiring "floating" gate. The shrine complex comprises a main hall, a noh theater stage, and a prayer hall, offering a glimpse into Japan's rich cultural heritage. While restoration work has been underway on the gate since 2019, a significant portion of the scaffolding has already been removed, with the complete restoration anticipated by the end of 2022.

Entry Fee: Adults ¥300, Highschool Students ¥200, Junior High and Elementary School Students ¥100

Location: 1-1 Miyajimacho, Hatsukaichi, Hiroshima 739-0588, Japan

Umeda Sky Building

Dominating the Kita district, the Umeda Sky Building stands tall as a remarkable high-rise structure, also referred to as the New Umeda City. Rising to a height of 173 meters, this architectural gem comprises two interconnected towers and boasts a subterranean restaurant. The observatory on the 39th floor provides a mesmerizing panoramic view of the city, guaranteeing an unforgettable experience.

Location: 1 Chome-1-88 Oyodonaka, Kita Ward, Osaka, 531-6023, Japan

Entry Fee (Observatory): Adults ¥1500, Children aged 4-12 ¥350

Hakone Open Air Museum

Nestled in Hakone, Japan's first outdoor museum, the Hakone Open Air Museum showcases an impressive collection of artistic masterpieces. Notable attractions include the Picasso Exhibition Hall, Symphonic Sculpture, and Zig Zag World. Immersed in the breathtaking beauty of the surrounding mountains, visitors can marvel at over 100 captivating works of art, creating a harmonious blend of nature and artistic expression.

Location: 1121 Ninotaira, Hakone, Ashigarashimo District, Kanagawa 250-0407, Japan

Entry Fee: Adults ¥1600, University and High School Students ¥1200, Middle and Elementary School Students ¥800

Georgia Tucker

GREAT OUTDOOR ACTIVITIES IN JAPAN

Japan has earned acclaim as a top destination for cultural exploration, historical immersion, and gastronomic delights. While many tourists are familiar with the country's remarkable hiking spots, there is a wealth of thrilling outdoor activities for adventurous travelers seeking an adrenaline rush. As an avid seeker of excitement myself, I have personally experienced a multitude of exhilarating outdoor pursuits in Japan. Here, I present a curated list of my top five favorites: quad riding, riverboarding (including rafting and tubing), wake surfing, horse riding, and free-flying.

An Exhilarating ATV Quad Ride

For those who enjoy recreational driving and don't mind a bit of mud, ATV biking is an ideal choice. This family-friendly activity allows children to accompany the driver, offering a memorable experience for all. As the courses are typically situated off-road, away from traffic, participants can revel in Japan's natural splendor. I personally engaged in this adventure and found it to be both physically demanding and thrilling. Our 1.5-hour course included an exciting segment through knee-deep water. While our group of approximately 20 individuals maintained a moderate speed of around 25km/h, ATV bikes can reach maximum speeds of approximately 50km/h, although speeds typically remain below 30km/h. To explore a variety of ATV experiences throughout Japan, visit the website mentioned.

Georgia Tucker

White Water Riverboarding

Riverboarding, also known as hydrospeed, ranks among the most exhilarating water activities I have ever encountered. While I have a profound affinity for water-related pursuits, I must admit that some moments during this experience evoked a sense of fear. Therefore, I recommend riverboarding primarily to individuals in good physical condition who possess a love for water and seek a more challenging alternative to rafting. The necessary safety gear, including a wetsuit, shoes, helmet, and life vest, ensures a secure adventure.

Utilizing a specialized floating foam board with a handhold, participants are provided instructions by a knowledgeable guide before embarking on their thrilling journey. Prepare for copious amounts of water, thrilling speeds, and moments where gripping tightly becomes essential. Opting for the half-day course proved to be ample for our group, allowing us to savor the captivating Tama River area afterward. For riverboarding tour reservations, please refer to the provided website.

Wake Surfing on a Never-Ending Wave

While my wakeboarding experience has been limited to cable wake parks, I am eager to check wake surfing off my list. Recently, I came across a television feature on wake surfing at Lake Yamanashi (Yamanashiko) in Japan. What makes it even more enticing is the breathtaking backdrop of Mt. Fuji while gliding across the water. It's hard to think of a more enjoyable way to spend a weekend day.

Just like wakeboarding, wake surfing requires practice to improve, but most individuals can manage to stand up during their first session. The aforementioned television segment even showed a comedian, who appeared to be out of shape, successfully standing up by the end of the session. Once you're on your feet, it's smooth sailing on the never-ending wave created by the boat. From that point forward, the experience is pure enjoyment. You can arrange a wake surfing experience in Yamanashiko through this website.

Horse Riding with a Sea View

Few things are as relaxing as horse riding while gazing upon the captivating cobalt-blue sea. Horse riding can be enjoyed in various locations outside major urban areas throughout Japan, and we had the opportunity to go riding in Yomitan, Okinawa. The remarkable aspect is that the Okinawa Riding Club not only offers beachside rides but also allows riders to venture into the sea alongside their horses.

Free Flying with Indoor Skydiving

Although it may not be an outdoor activity, indoor skydiving is an exhilarating experience worth mentioning. If you're not yet ready for an actual outdoor skydive but still yearn to feel the thrill of freefall and flight, you can try indoor skydiving at FlyStation in Koshigaya, Saitama (north of Tokyo).

After donning a special suit designed to facilitate floating in the wind, the staff will provide detailed explanations of the upcoming experience. You'll also have the opportunity to practice on dry land before entering the wind tunnel for your flight. Powerful gusts of wind will elevate you, and depending on your skills, you can even attempt tricks. While the cost of this experience is not modest, at 4,500 yen per minute (5,000 yen on weekends), the unique and extraordinary sensation makes it worthwhile. Children as young as 4 years old can participate, and the weight limit is set at 125kg.

THE TOP 10 BEACHES IN JAPAN
Japan boasts captivating beaches that rival the best in the world.

Georgia Tucker

Glistening under the radiant sunlight, Japan's beaches offer endless stretches of cobalt blue sea and pristine white sand. Surprisingly, Japan is home to photogenic beaches where you can immerse yourself in an exotic tropical atmosphere and rejuvenate your mind and body. The ideal season for swimming in the sea is from July to September. For those interested in diving and snorkeling, you'll discover vibrant coral reefs teeming with colorful fish. Visiting Japan's beach resorts is an experience that should not be missed.

1. Nishihama, Okinawa

Lose yourself in "Hateruma Blue" in the southernmost town of Japan

Good for:

- Families

- Couples
- Budget
- Photo

A boat ride of approximately an hour and a half from Ishigaki Island will take you to Hateruma Island, Okinawa, the southernmost inhabited island in Japan. On the northern part of the island, near Hateruma Port, lies Nishihama, a stunning beach. Interestingly, "Nishi" means north in the local dialect. The sea shimmering in the distinctive "Hateruma Blue" hue is truly unforgettable. The beach offers public amenities such as showers, toilets, and an observation deck.

Location: Hateruma, Taketomi-cho, Yaeyama-gun, Okinawa 907-1751, Japan

2. Yonaha Beach, Okinawa
Miyakojima's extensive stretch of white sandy beach ranks among the finest in the Orient.

Good for:

• Families

• Couples

• Budget travelers

• Photography enthusiasts

Yonaha Maehama, also known as "Maipama Beach," in Miyakojima is immensely popular among both locals and tourists from Japan and around the world. The beach's pristine white sands span 7 kilometers, creating a striking contrast against the shimmering cobalt blue sea. It is also an excellent destination for water sports enthusiasts.

Location: 1199 Yonaha, Shimoji, Miyakojima City, Okinawa 906-0000, Japan

3. Sunayama Beach, Okinawa

Amazing views and natural rock arches at one of Miyakojima's best beaches

Good for:

- Families
- Couples
- Budget
- Photo

Ideal for families, couples, those on a budget, and photography enthusiasts, this beach provides a splendid opportunity to relish the exquisite evening scenery. The renowned arched rock offers breathtaking views of the sky, sea, and the enchanting illumination of the setting sun. Nature's splendor is truly unparalleled in this location. Moreover, visitors can avail themselves of gear rental shops and enjoy light meals and beverages. Conveniently located near Miyakojima's city center, the site offers easy accessibility and amenities such as showers and a parking area.

Location: Miyakojima City, Okinawa 906-0000, Japan

4. Furuzamami Beach, Okinawa

Snorkeling in the crystal-clear sea of Michelin-starred Zamami

Georgia Tucker

Good for:

- Families
- Couples
- Budget
- Photo

Nestled in the southern part of Zamami Island, Furuzamami Beach beckons visitors with its crystal-clear seas, earning it a coveted two-star rating in the Michelin Green Guide Japan. This remote island, easily accessible on a day trip from the main island of Okinawa, offers an underwater paradise adorned with vibrant coral reefs teeming with tropical fish.

Ideal for families, couples, those on a budget, and photography enthusiasts, this beach is a haven for divers and snorkelers. Delight in the breathtakingly clear azure waters that extend as far as the eye can see. Furuzamami Beach serves as Zamami Island's primary beach and promises an unforgettable experience.

Location: 1743 Zamami Village, Shimajiri District, Okinawa 901-3402, Japan

5. Hate-No-Hama, Okinawa

The Okinawan dream: sail to an uninhabited island of sandy beaches

Good for:

- Families
- Couples
- Budget
- Photo

Perfect for families, couples, those on a budget, and photography enthusiasts, this island comprises three picturesque sandy beaches—Maine Beach, Nakano Beach, and Hate Beach. With its long and narrow white sandy shores and surrounding blue and transparent waters, this destination transports visitors to a realm seemingly detached from reality. Be sure not to miss the breathtaking sunsets that grace the horizon. Access to the island is typically facilitated by tour boats, allowing for an array of activities such as snorkeling, diving, and marine sports. Yet, the true allure lies in immersing oneself in the extraordinary serenity of the surroundings—an idyllic haven where sea and sand converge in tranquil harmony.

Location: Kumejima-cho, Shimajiri-gun, Okinawa 901-3100, Japan

6. Okinawa Kondoi Beach

A famous sunset spot on Taketomi Island with a "phantom beach"

Good for:

- Families
- Couples
- Budget
- Photo

Catering to families, couples, those on a budget, and photography enthusiasts, this beach on Taketomi Island captivates visitors of all ages with its shallow and serene waters. It stands as the sole beach on the island, offering mesmerizing views of Iriomote Island, Kohama Island, and Kuro Island. Traverse the sandbar and experience the magical phenomenon of the "phantom beach" revealed during low tide, evoking a true castaway sensation. Immerse yourself in cherished moments with your loved ones amidst this captivating environment.

Location: Taketomi-cho, Yaeyama-gun, Okinawa 907-1101, Japan

7. Hirizo Beach, Shizuoka

The southernmost part of Izu is a certified Geopark with untouched beauty

Good for:

- Families
- Couples
- Budget
- Photo

Ideal for families, couples, those on a budget, and photography enthusiasts, this secluded beach is not easily accessible by land. Ferry transportation to the tents set up in Nakagi is available exclusively during the summertime. Brimming with coral clusters submerged in pristine, crystal-clear waters and teeming with an array of colorful fish, this destination has gained popularity among snorkeling enthusiasts. Embark on a seaside adventure encompassed by the breathtaking natural surroundings, and revel in the unparalleled splendor of Nakagi.

Location: Nakagi, Minamiizu Town, Kamo District, Shizuoka Prefecture 415-0311, Japan

8. Wakayama Shirarahama
Parasols sway in the sea breeze at this tropical Wakayama resort

Good for:

- Families
- Couples
- Budget
- Photo

Perfect for families, couples, those on a budget, and photography enthusiasts, this beach, akin to its sister beach Waikiki Beach in Honolulu, Hawaii, stretches for approximately 620 meters. It holds immense popularity among swimmers during the summer months, with the vibrant parasols adorning the beach creating a captivating sight. The sand here, consisting of 90% silicic acid quartz, offers a remarkably smooth texture underfoot. Revel in the translucent seawater, which provides an ideal backdrop for leisurely aquatic activities, creating an idyllic coastal sanctuary. Furthermore, be sure to explore the local culinary delights, adding a culinary dimension to your visit.

Location: 864 Shirahama-cho, Nishimuro-gun, Wakayama 649-2211, Japan

9. KAGOSHIMA TOMORI BEACH
A beach with blue sea locally acclaimed as the "Blue Angel"

Good for:

- Families
- Couples
- Budget
- Photo

Nestled along the Tomori coastline lies the "Galapagos of the Orient," a gracefully curved beach highly regarded as Kagoshima's and Amami Oshima's finest. Aptly referred to as the "Blue Angel," the sea's color magically transforms into varying shades of blue throughout the day. The serene and placid surface of the water provides a soothing visual experience. With convenient accessibility from Amami Airport, this beach is an ideal destination for sightseeing.

Location: Oaza Ujuku, Kasari-cho, Amami City, Kagoshima Prefecture 894-0501, Japan

10. YURIGAHAMA, KAGOSHIMA

Take a trip to this white beach off the coast of Yoron Island to collect lucky star-shaped sand

Good for:

- Families
- Couples
- Budget
- Photo

As the largest beach on Yoron Island, Yurigahama emerges only during low tide (from the half tide to the spring tide) along the coast of Oganeku. The allure of this place reaches its pinnacle as the crystal-clear water sparkles in the warm sunshine. You can reach the beach by boat or personal watercraft. Legend has it that collecting star sand grains, one for each year of your age, brings happiness. Why not seize the opportunity? Immerse yourself in the wonders of nature within this enchanting setting.

Georgia Tucker

Location: Furusato Oaza, Yoron-cho, Oshima-gun, Kagoshima Prefecture 891-9307, Japan

Georgia Tucker

CHAPTER ELEVEN

SAFETY IN JAPAN

RISKS AND DANGERS IN JAPAN

Japan boasts a beautiful and diverse environment, with over 70% of its land being mountainous and varying climates from subarctic in the north to subtropical in the south. With more than 200 volcanoes and 6,852 islands, the country offers a plethora of stunning habitats to explore, but it also comes with a range of potential risks.

Natural Disasters

Japan experiences its share of natural disasters, including earthquakes, tsunamis, volcanic eruptions, typhoons, and landslides. Fortunately, the country has established robust public warning systems and evacuation procedures. Your accommodation provider should provide information about natural disasters and the appropriate protocols to follow in such events. It is advisable to stay informed about local weather warnings or advisories from the Japan Meteorological Agency before and during your trip.

Certain regions are more susceptible to specific natural disasters. Earthquakes are more prevalent in the northeast, while Okinawa, Hokkaido, and Kyushu are prone to typhoons.

Always consult the government's international travel advisory before making any travel arrangements. Japan has an earthquake early warning system in place, which triggers alarms in the event of a major earthquake. These alarms range from chimes to air raid sirens. Different procedures apply depending on whether you are indoors or outdoors. The Japan National Tourism Organization offers online safety tips for travelers on how to respond during an earthquake.

Fukushima Power Plant

The devastating Great East Japan earthquake and subsequent tsunami in March 2011 caused significant destruction in northeast Japan, despite the presence of sea wall defenses. Since then, the affected cities and towns have been restored to their original state and have resumed their bustling activities.

However, a radiation exclusion zone remains in effect around the Fukushima Dai-Ichi nuclear power plant in Fukushima Prefecture, northeast Honshu. It is important not to travel to areas with warnings or exclusions in place. Presently, Hiroshima and Nagasaki do not have radiation warnings and are safe to visit.

Animals And Insects

In Japan, overall safety from dangerous animals is relatively high, particularly if your itinerary primarily focuses on urban areas. The country is home to remarkable creatures, such as the renowned wild snow monkeys near Nagano. However, it is essential to remember that these animals are wild and may resort to biting if they feel threatened. Therefore, it is advisable to maintain a safe distance unless instructed by a guide to approach closely.

When venturing into rural regions, it is prudent to wear appropriate footwear, such as hiking boots, as a precautionary measure. This ensures preparedness in encountering less desirable fauna. Notable creatures to be cautious of include giant centipedes, venomous snakes, and the Denki mushi—a small green caterpillar capable of delivering an electric shock-like sensation upon contact.

Among Japan's most lethal creatures are giant hornets, which have unfortunately caused fatalities. Their venom possesses potent toxicity, posing a significant risk even to non-allergic individuals. If stung, it is crucial to seek immediate medical assistance. Giant hornets are typically observed during the summer months in rural areas. When approaching locations with a high hornet population, warning signs are usually visible, prompting the wise decision to avoid such areas due to the increased likelihood of encountering nests and subsequent stings. Conduct thorough research on the specific region you plan to visit and activities you intend to engage in, such as ocean encounters or mountain hikes, to ascertain any potential threats from animals or insects.

Crime

Although Japan is widely regarded as a safe destination for tourists, exercising common sense is paramount to avoid trouble. Implementing a few simple precautions can significantly contribute to your safety while traveling:

• Refrain from venturing alone at night into quiet or poorly lit areas, particularly if you are unfamiliar with the surroundings.

- Be mindful of potential instances of bag snatching and ensure that your valuables are securely concealed, kept close to your person, and zipped up.

- Limit the amount of cash carried at any given time. Distribute funds between a hotel safe, wallet, and a secure pocket to minimize loss in the event of theft or pickpocketing.

- Prioritize research or consult trustworthy sources, such as the hotel concierge, to identify any unsafe areas to avoid within your designated district.

- Maintain constant vigilance over your drink and never leave it unattended. Exercise caution when accepting food or beverages from strangers unless you witness the drink being poured by a bartender or served by a waiter.

- Refrain from disclosing personal details, including your accommodation, and exercise caution when approached by individuals seeking unnecessary personal information.

Local Laws
Japan encompasses certain laws and customs that may come as a surprise to foreigners. Familiarizing yourself with these basic regulations will help prevent inadvertent violations:

- Be mindful of no smoking signs, as smoking in public is prohibited in certain areas, and offenders may face fines.

- Consumption of alcohol in public spaces is legally permissible in Japan, with vending machines even selling beer and sake. However, it is crucial to display respectful behavior and avoid drawing unnecessary attention when consuming alcoholic beverages in parks or on beaches. It is important to note that the legal drinking age is 20, and adherence to this regulation is strictly enforced by Japanese authorities.

• Japan maintains a zero percent blood-alcohol limit for driving, even if the consumption occurs on a previous day. Thus, if planning to operate a vehicle, it is imperative to abstain from alcohol consumption.

• Carrying your passport at all times while traveling within Japan is mandatory, as law enforcement authorities may request to inspect it. Failure to comply with this requirement could lead to potential arrest.

• Law enforcement officials possess the authority to conduct stop and search procedures, seize illegal items, and detain individuals without charge for up to 23 days.

• It is essential to be aware that certain prescription drugs purchased abroad may be deemed illegal in Japan. If you require medication during your visit, ensure that you possess a prescription note from your doctor and carry a letter explaining the necessity of the medication.

COMMON CLAIMS
Extreme Weather
Instances of travelers being stranded at their destination for an extended period or unable to reach their intended location due to typhoons and snowstorms are not uncommon. While such events are often unforeseen, there are measures you can take to mitigate the impact. We recommend purchasing a Single Trip

insurance policy as soon as you book your flights and accommodation. Alternatively, if you opt for an Annual Multi-Trip policy, ensure that the start date coincides with your travel bookings. This way, if your trip is canceled before your departure, your pre-paid expenses will be covered. Furthermore, in the event of extended stays overseas due to flight cancellations, we can provide coverage for accommodation and related expenses, preventing financial burdens.

Snow Injuries
We frequently receive claims from travelers requiring medical care following ski or snowboarding accidents. In addition to medical expenses, there may be costs associated with cutting the trip short to facilitate an early return for treatment. To alleviate stress in such situations, it is advisable to obtain appropriate coverage. When purchasing a policy with Southern Cross Travel Insurance, you have the option to include skiing and snowboarding cover for an additional fee.

16 TIPS FOR HOW TO SAVE MONEY IN JAPAN WHEN TRAVELLING JAPAN!

Japan is renowned for its high cost of living, but this should not deter you from visiting if you have a genuine desire to experience the country. Having backpacked through Japan for 2.5 weeks, I discovered that it is indeed possible to explore Japan on a budget and find ways to save money. Whether you are already in Japan or planning your trip, this Japan travel blog and guide presents several tips for cost-effective travel within the country.

TRANSPORT IN JAPAN ON A BUDGET

1. Get A Jr Pass & Be Clever with How You Use It.

You may have heard about the necessity of a JR Pass for traveling within Japan, especially if you plan to visit multiple cities within a limited timeframe. Read this post to understand why it can be a money-saving option. While JR Passes may initially seem expensive, you can optimize their value by using them cleverly. For instance, choose a 7-day, 14-day, or 21-day pass based on your travel needs. During my 18-day trip, I purchased the 14-day pass since I did not require it for the first two days in Osaka and the last days in Tokyo. This decision saved me £80.00, the price difference between the 14-day and 21-day JR Passes at the time of purchase. In addition to intercity travel, the JR Pass can be used for day trips, reducing transportation costs.

For example, taking day trips to Nara and Kyoto from Osaka, where accommodations are more affordable!

2. Use the Jr Rail Lines Within Cities as Much As Possible.

The JR Pass is not limited to Bullet Trains (Shinkansen) in Japan. Cities like Kobe, Kyoto, and Tokyo have JR Train Lines running through them alongside subway and metro systems. These JR Lines are marked in train stations and maps. By taking advantage of these JR Lines, you can travel within the cities by simply showing your valid JR Pass to the inspectors at the gates. No additional tickets or charges are required, as they are covered by the pass. During my three-day exploration of Tokyo, I exclusively used JR Lines, resulting in zero transportation expenses—a remarkable way to save money in Japan!

3. Refund Your Icoca Card.

To navigate non-JR Lines or areas without a valid JR Pass, such as Osaka, Kyoto, Kobe, Nara, and Hiroshima, an ICOCA Card is essential. This reloadable card costs 2000 yen initially, and it includes 1500 yen of transport credit and a 500 yen deposit for the card. To save some money in Japan, remember to visit a ticket office before leaving the Kansai region and request a refund of the 500 yen deposit and any remaining credit on the card.

ACCOMMODATION IN JAPAN ON A BUDGET

4. Book Accommodation Near a Jr Station.

If you prefer using JR Lines with your JR Pass to travel within cities without incurring extra costs, it is advisable to book accommodations near JR Line stations. This eliminates the need to take subways from non-JR stations to reach your lodging, saving money on transportation expenses. Many hostels in Japan explicitly mention their proximity to JR Lines in their descriptions on platforms like Booking.com, or guests often mention it in their reviews.

5. Book A Hostel in Japan & Book A Big Dorm.

Japan offers a plethora of well-designed hostels that have gained popularity as affordable alternatives to hotels. Based on my personal experience, hostels in Japan provide an excellent accommodation option. To optimize cost savings, consider staying in a large dormitory room, which tends to offer the most budget-friendly rates. It is worth noting that some hostels advertise dormitories with up to 56 beds, although I find this arrangement quite extensive. Nevertheless, to ensure frugality during your stay in Japan, prioritize booking larger dormitories. Remember to pack essentials such as an eye mask and earplugs for a comfortable rest.

MEALS IN JAPAN ON A BUDGET.

6. Eat Breakfast at Your Hostel.

Finding breakfast options can often be challenging, as they tend to be expensive when procured from cafes or restaurants. Additionally, locating open establishments can prove problematic. Thankfully, many hostels in Japan are equipped with kitchens, providing the convenience of preparing your breakfast. Consider purchasing bread, eggs, cereal, or milk upon arrival at the hostel to save money on breakfast expenses. Additionally, some hostels include breakfast as part of their rates, making it an appealing cost-saving option.

7. Make Use of Supermarket Food.
Japanese supermarkets, particularly 7/11 and Family Mart, offer a wide selection of high-quality food options. These establishments boast an extensive range of sushi, ranging from individual pieces to complete boxes. Moreover, they provide pre-made Japanese meals, which can be consumed cold or heated. Remarkably, these meals often present an appealing alternative at a fraction of the cost compared to even modest restaurants. As mentioned earlier, most hostels in Japan feature kitchens, enabling guests to heat meals instead of dining out for every meal. In the absence of kitchen facilities, 7/11 and Family Mart provide microwaves, and some supermarkets even offer seating areas where you can enjoy your meal.

8. Eat Street Food in Japan.
Japan is renowned for its delectable street food offerings, which can be savored in various popular areas and cities. From savory treats like Mochi (Japanese Rice Cakes) and a variety of rice cakes to iconic dishes like beef, Takoyaki (Octopus Balls), Okonomi Yaki, and a plethora of noodles, the street food scene in Japan promises a memorable culinary adventure.

9. Don't Eat in The Touristy Areas.
Although it may seem obvious, it is worth emphasizing the importance of avoiding touristy areas when seeking to save money while dining in Japan. Popular tourist hubs like Dotonbori in Osaka and Harajuku in Tokyo, with their impressive signage and enticing restaurants, often come with higher price tags. To minimize expenses, venture beyond these areas and explore local

eateries. On my first day in Osaka, I was taken aback by an unexpectedly higher bill. Although the menu displayed reasonable prices, I was required to order a drink, which is not typically the case for me, and taxes were added at the end, significantly increasing the total cost. Such occurrences are less common outside major tourist zones and streets. Furthermore, it is advisable to steer clear of animal cafes in Japan due to ethical concerns, as these establishments tend to be expensive and raise additional reasons to avoid them.

10. Get Coffee from The Vending Machines.

If you have a penchant for coffee, consider bypassing Starbucks and other coffee chains in Japan. Instead, make use of the ubiquitous vending machines scattered throughout the country to save money. These machines offer an assortment of beverages, including various types of coffee and tea, with the added convenience of hot options for those seeking warmth during the winter months. Not only are vending machine coffees priced significantly lower than those offered in coffee shops, but the experience of using these machines also adds a touch of novelty to your journey.

11. Consider the Tax or Look for Tax-Free Shops.

Be mindful that prices displayed in Japan often exclude taxes, which can lead to unexpected expenditures. Always verify whether tax is included or not to accurately calculate the final price. Additionally, be on the lookout for tax-free shops, as they can provide opportunities to save money on certain purchases.

12. Look Out for Free Things to Do in Japan.
As with any country or city, Japan offers a multitude of paid activities. However, I discovered a range of exceptional free things to do in Japan, including exploring parks and fascinating neighborhoods that can occupy several days of your itinerary without incurring any expenses.

13. Consider the Time of Year You Visit Japan.
During my visit to Japan, I experienced the captivating Cherry Blossom Season in spring, which coincided with increased accommodation prices. If you seek a budget-friendly trip to Japan, consider visiting during winter, as it offers lower tourist footfall and more affordable lodging options. While summer is also a favorable time to visit, it can be quite hot. I highly recommend researching accommodation options throughout the year before finalizing your flight bookings to avoid peak season periods. Booking.com was my preferred platform for securing accommodations in Japan, offering flexible booking options that allow for changes closer to your travel dates without incurring cancellation fees.

14. Fly into One City And Out Of Another.
A strategy that significantly contributed to my cost savings was flying into Kansai Airport, which serves Osaka, Kyoto, and Kobe, and departing from Tokyo Airport. This approach not only reduced the cost of my flights (as it was more economical to fly from Taiwan to Osaka than Taiwan to Tokyo), but it also eliminated the need for backtracking. As mentioned earlier, using

the JR Pass intelligently is crucial for saving money in Japan. Towards the end of my trip to Tokyo, my JR Pass had expired, requiring me to pay for a train from Tokyo Station to the airport. However, had I booked a flight departing from Osaka, I would have needed a valid JR Pass until closer to the end of my trip and might have needed to purchase a 21-day pass instead of a 14-day pass. To find the best deals, I utilized Skyscanner to compare various dates and routes for my flights to and from Japan.

15. Take A Free Walking Tour.

Having a knowledgeable guide to navigate and provide insights into your surroundings is always enriching, albeit often accompanied by a fee. This is where free walking tours come into play. Japan offers numerous free walking tours, particularly in Tokyo and Osaka. Upon arrival, I recommend exploring these options, as they offer exceptional value as free activities in Japan. It's important to note that while these tours are advertised as free, it is customary to provide a tip at the end if you enjoyed the experience. Nevertheless, they remain a budget-friendly alternative to full-priced tours.

16. Shop Around for The Best Sim Card.

Obtaining a sim card in Japan can be relatively costly compared to other countries, making it less favorable for cost-conscious travelers seeking to save money. During my trip, I purchased a 3GB Travel Sim Card in Japan for approximately £20.00, which I utilized within a week. Consequently, I continued my journey without a sim card, relying solely on Wi-Fi availability. There are options for acquiring a 10GB sim card for around £35.00 or renting a Wi-Fi Pocket Router daily. However, I found the Wi-Fi connectivity in my hostels to be excellent, and certain cities like Osaka provided public Wi-Fi access in stations. Although Tokyo had limited public Wi-Fi options, most cafes and restaurants offered Wi-Fi services, ultimately lessening the need for continuous Internet access.

CONCLUSION

We hope that "The In-Depth Japan Travel Guide 2023-2024" has given you a taste of what this amazing country has to offer. From the bustling streets of Tokyo to the tranquil forests of Nara, from the ski slopes of Hokkaido to the beaches of Okinawa, Japan is a place of contrasts and surprises that will leave you in awe.

We understand that traveling to Japan can seem daunting, especially for those on a budget. But with the tips, advice, and recommendations in this guide, we hope to show you that a trip to Japan can be affordable, accessible, and unforgettable.

As you plan your trip, remember to keep an open mind and be ready to embrace the unexpected. Try new foods, explore new neighborhoods, and immerse yourself in the local culture. And don't forget to take advantage of the many free or low-cost attractions that Japan has to offer, from public parks and gardens to temples and shrines.

We hope that "The In-Depth Japan Travel Guide 2023-2024" has inspired you to plan your adventure to this incredible country. Whether you're a solo traveler, a couple, or a family, Japan has something for everyone, and we guarantee that you'll come away from your trip with memories that will last a lifetime.

So, pack your bags, book your flights, and get ready to experience a Japan that will blow your mind. We wish you safe travels, and we can't wait to hear about your own "In Depth" Japan travel experience.

Georgia Tucker

Made in United States
Troutdale, OR
09/14/2023

12916737R00184